ENDO

"I wish I had this book in my first year of marriage! *Hot, Holy, and Humorous* is a great resource for wives who desire to learn more about sex within the covenant of marriage. This book is for a mature audience, packed full of knowledge and inspiration, equipping wives to embrace this intimate part of marriage that God designed."

—**Jennifer Smith**, author of *The Unveiled Wife* and founder of UnveiledWife.com

"Passionate lovemaking—isn't that your heart's desire? Invest in yourself and your marriage with J. Parker's lovemaking guide for Christian wives! Biblical and full of practical suggestions, this book offers you an exciting pathway to authentic sexual intimacy."

—**Julie Sibert**, speaker, author, and blogger at IntimacyInMarriage.com

"Who said sex can't be both hot and holy? Certainly not J. Parker, who has made it her life's mission to change the way Christian women see sex. God made it awesome—and if it's not that way for you yet, J. Parker shows you how you can find the 'hot wife' inside you!"

—**Sheila Wray Gregoire**, author of *The Good Girl's Guide to Great Sex* and blogger at ToLoveHonorandVacuum.com

"Hurray for J. Parker's new release *Hot, Holy, and Humorous*! A few years ago while reading her blog of the same name, we had an epiphany for our sexual relationship. We are delighted that she included that particular little tidbit (you'll have to guess which one!) along with much other valuable, practical information in this great book. Put her advice into practice and you will enjoy some added sizzle in *your* marriage bed."

—**Dr. Dan and Linda Wilson**, authors of *Lovemaking: 10 Secrets to Extravagant Intimacy in Marriage*, and co-founders of Supernatural Marriage and Missions, SupernaturalMarriage.net

Drink your fill!
Song of Songs 5:1

HOT, HOLY, and HUMOROUS

Sex in Marriage by God's Design

J. PARKER

J Parker

BroadStreet
PUBLISHING

BroadStreet Publishing Group, LLC
Racine, Wisconsin, USA
BroadStreetPublishing.com

HOT, HOLY, and HUMOROUS
Sex in Marriage by God's Design

ISBN-13: 978-1-4245-5240-5 (softcover)
ISBN-13: 978-1-4245-5241-2 (e-book)

Cover design by GarborgDesign.com
Interior design and typeset by Katherine Lloyd, theDESKonline.com
Illustrations by Matt Baxter

Printed in the United States of America

16 17 18 19 20 5 4 3 2 1

To my beloved husband.
We belong together.

My beloved is mine and I am his.

Song of Songs 2:16

CONTENTS

PREFACE

Thirty years ago, if you'd gone looking for a book on sexuality from a Christian perspective, you wouldn't have found much. A few bold individuals had tackled the subject, and more had included a single chapter on sexual intimacy in a book on marriage. But resources were still sparse.

Today, thankfully, you can find many more Christian books about sexuality. Physicians, nurses, professors, theologians, ministers, professional speakers, and others offer excellent treatment of God's biblical plan for physical intimacy. So why provide another?

When I began blogging at Hot, Holy & Humorous, I took a somewhat different approach. While most Christian books on sexuality address anatomy, theology, attitude, and answers for specific problems, many wives are also looking for specifics on *how*—how to have an orgasm, how to try new sexual positions, how to get in the mood, etc. There are secular resources for this approach, but not much from Christian authors.

Just as we're commanded by God to love, sometimes we need to know what that looks like in a particular situation—how to better handle a coworker, or parent a child, or reach out to a friend. Likewise, we wives want concrete tips on what it looks like to show physical love in marriage according to God's design.

In my blog, I primarily focus on the kind of information and encouragement you'd get from a best friend over a cup of coffee—you know, a gal-pal who offers helpful advice and the low-down on the low-down.

Hot, Holy, and Humorous: Sex in Marriage by God's Design is a compilation of that advice. Let's sit together, girlfriend, and let me share my heart and wisdom with you on this issue.

You can read this book from front to back or simply pick out the chapters that interest or apply to you. It's not your standard sex book, or even a typical Christian sex book. It's straight talk with a foundation of faith and a splash of humor.

I pray that *Hot, Holy, and Humorous* helps Christian wives by giving biblical and blunt tips on how to have a sex life that goes the distance and honors our heavenly Father.

–J

Chapter 1
CULTIVATING ROMANCE

Odds are that at some point in your relationship, your husband was romantic. Maybe it didn't come naturally and maybe it was only at the beginning, but something he did made you swoon a little.

Keeping romance alive has been the subject of plenty of self-help books, blogs, magazine articles, movies, and more. I'm not the truest romantic myself (for instance, I usually prefer action films to chick flicks), but I agree that romance is an important aspect of marriage. So how do you keep that spark alive? Let's delve into non-romantic husbands and love letters.

If you find my love,
tell him that I am lovesick.
Song of Solomon 5:8 (HCSB)

When He's Not Romantic

I am married to Spock. Have you heard of him? He's the Vulcan character from the original *Star Trek* series (and recent movie reboot of the story). The defining characteristic of the Vulcan species is their ability to suppress emotion and focus entirely on what is logical.

Yep, that's my husband: *logical.*

Bringing your wife flowers for no reason is not logical. Buying expensive jewelry because it's pretty is not logical. Telling her that she's beautiful today when you already said it last week is not logical.

I'm not the only one married to someone who doesn't "get it" when it comes to beauty, spontaneity, and going the extra mile for a big gesture of love. So how do you get a guy like this to engage in romance in your marriage?

Here's what I've learned from my marriage to a Vulcan:

Take the lead. It does not occur to my husband to create a romantic environment for date night or lovemaking. Since I am the one who craves romance more—even though he does enjoy it—I take it upon myself to set the scene. I light the candles, I turn on the music, I pour the bubble bath. Putting forth a little effort can create an atmosphere where the only instruction left is simply "Add Hubby."

Ask for romance. I need to hear that I am beautiful, that my husband desires me, that he loves me. Sometimes he forgets that. I used to be hurt by the omission. But after several years of marriage, I realized my husband doesn't gush about his mother either, and she is downright heroic to him.

Rather than feeling injured by his inattention, I invite his attention. For instance, I can put on my sexy nightie (or nudie) and ask, "So, what do you think?" Or say, "You know what I like about your body?" and go through a list, followed by "What do you like about mine?" That opens the floor for him to express what I need to hear.

Establish routines. I had a friend whose husband's lack of affection hurt her feelings. She finally told him, "I need you to kiss me before you leave for work and kiss me when you get home." It became their routine. Was it forced at first? Yeah, a little. But now it's something they both enjoy—a romantic tradition.

Demanding lots of spontaneous romance from a non-romantic guy is like starting a Mount Everest expedition with a few Kit-Kat bars in your backpack. Don't get your hopes up! Asking your honey to introduce a romantic routine into your relationship, though, is predictable and tangible—something he can put on a to-do list and check off.

Perhaps the routine is a kiss or a hug at a certain time. Maybe he plans a date or a vacation for the two of you on a special day each year (giving him plenty of time to prepare). The routine might be that he undresses you in a particular way, noting as he goes along all the beautiful parts of your body.

Romantic routines can be great for both of you. Just make the tradition something achievable for him and enjoyable to you.

Remember your husband loves you. When your best friend tells you how her romantic hubby swept her off her feet with a surprise trip to a secluded cabin where he cooked her favorite meal, serenaded her with his guitar, and sprinkled the bed with rose petals before making love to her, you may wonder why your husband doesn't love you like that.

While I encourage husbands to up their game when it comes to the romance department, some guys are amazing at it and some guys aren't. Whether your mate has natural wooing talent is not related to how much he loves you.

Plenty of non-romantic guys would respond to "Do you love your wife?" with an unequivocal "Of course." In fact, it isn't logical to Mr. Spock to restate the obvious over and over. So ask your husband to *tell* you and to *show* you, and when he follows through, remember that he is outside his comfort zone in expressing the love for you that is well within his comfort zone. He loves you like crazy; he just needs cues from you for how to demonstrate that love.

Enjoy the surprises. Since my guy isn't a hard-core romantic, I revel in those times when he goes above and beyond. For a recent birthday, he wrote me a love poem. A love poem! If you knew this guy—which you do if you've ever watched the original *Star Trek*—you'd know how big a deal that is. I was on Cloud 9½ for the next month.

We wives should all enjoy the romance our husbands bring to marriage, but when it's not your guy's thing, those moments are super-sweet. Instead of thinking, *I wish he would do this more often*, just enjoy the moment. Bask in it. Know how hard it was for him to make that effort, and how much that means he loves you.

Wives, do what you can to introduce the romance you want into your marriage. Your husband likely won't be as romantic as the hunk in the latest chick flick. He doesn't have a screenwriting team to come up with all those great ideas for him. He's on his own. So help him out.

I can honestly say from my life with Spock that melding minds is far outweighed by melding hearts. And that can happen when we make the extra effort. (Plus, aren't those pointy ears kind of cute?)

How to Write a Love Letter

The best gift my husband ever gave me, hands-down, is the love poem he wrote. Now, it would likely have made Cyrano de Bergerac cringe and yank the pen out of his hand. But it was absolutely beautiful to me because it required effort and thought as he expressed how much I mean to him.

Making an effort to express your love on paper can mean so much to your beloved. But since we are not all as naturally romantic as Robert and Elizabeth Barrett Browning (who traded love poems with verses like "How do I love thee? Let me count the ways"[1]), I thought I'd give some tips for writing a love letter. Below are some components you might want to include.

Remember when? Recall a special memory you two shared. You could talk about when you first met or when you first knew your husband was The One and how that moment made you feel. Provide enough descriptive detail to re-create the scene and the emotions it evoked. Your memory could be romantic, funny, or a tale of triumph over hardship, as long as it's something that makes you both remember your courtship or marriage in a positive way.

Here are some samples:

> I look back to the early days of our acquaintance; and Friendship, as to the days of Love and Innocence; and with an undiscribable pleasure I have seen near a score of years roll over our Heads, with an affection heightend and improved by time—nor have the dreary years of absence in the smallest degree effaced from my mind the of the dear, untittled man to whom I gave my Heart.[2]
>
> —Abigail Adams to her husband,
> US President John Adams

All night long on my bed
  I looked for the one my heart loves;
  I looked for him but did not find him.
I will get up now and go about the city,
  through its streets and squares;
I will search for the one my heart loves.
  So I looked for him but did not find him.

The watchmen found me
  as they made their rounds in the city.
  "Have you seen the one my heart loves?"
Scarcely had I passed them
  when I found the one my heart loves.
I held him and would not let him go.

—Song of Songs 3:1–4

The best is yet to come. Write about your anticipation of the future with your beloved. What do you look forward to sharing with him? Is there something specific you've talked about in your future? Traveling? Settling down somewhere special? Making love in the living room after the kids grow up and move out? Whatever it is, let your husband know that you expect to be with him for a long time and are devoted to making your life together a good one.

Here are some examples:

> I will cover you with love when next I see you, with caresses, with ecstasy. I want to gorge you with all the joys of the flesh, so that you faint and die. I want you to be amazed by me, and to confess to yourself that you had never dreamed of such transports. … When you are old, I want you to recall those few hours, I want your dry bones to quiver with joy when you think of them.
>
> —Gustave Flaubert (author) to his wife, Louise Colet[3]

> Let us hope and believe that we shall walk hand in hand down the lengthening highway of life, one in heart, one in impulse & one in love & worship of Him—bearing each other's burdens, sharing each other's joys, soothing

each other's griefs—&, so linked together, & so journeying, pass at last the shadowed boundaries of Time & stand redeemed & saved, beyond the threshold & within the light of that Land whose Prince is the Lord of rest eternal.

—Mark Twain (Samuel Clemens) to his wife, Olivia Langdon[4]

What turns you on? We all want to feel attractive to our mates, so describe what features of your husband's appearance appeal to you. What about his looks turns you on? Avoid the basic "You're handsome" or "You're hot" statements, and get specific. Name parts of the body (eyes, mouth, legs, toenails, whatever) and tell what you like about them.

Samples:

How beautiful you are, my darling!
   Oh, how beautiful!
   Your eyes behind your veil are doves.
Your hair is like a flock of goats
   descending from the hills of Gilead.
Your teeth are like a flock of sheep just shorn,
   coming up from the washing.
Each has its twin;
   not one of them is alone.
Your lips are like a scarlet ribbon;
   your mouth is lovely.
Your temples behind your veil
   are like the halves of a pomegranate.
Your neck is like the tower of David,
   built with courses of stone;
on it hang a thousand shields,
   all of them shields of warriors.

Your two breasts are like two fawns,
  like twin fawns of a gazelle
  that browse among the lilies.

—Song of Songs 4:1–5

My beloved is radiant and ruddy,
  outstanding among ten thousand.
His head is purest gold;
  his hair is wavy
  and black as a raven.
His eyes are like doves
  by the water streams,
washed in milk,
  mounted like jewels.
His cheeks are like beds of spice
  yielding perfume.
His lips are like lilies
  dripping with myrrh.
His arms are rods of gold
  set with topaz.
His body is like polished ivory
  decorated with lapis lazuli.

—Song of Songs 5:10–14

The beauty within. No one wants to feel like they are only appreciated for their appearance. Sure, we want to be beautiful—but we also want our beauty to go deeper. God has given your man some special qualities that you appreciate, so name them. Is your honey humorous? Trustworthy? Smart? Handy? Generous? A good father? Consider pointing out specific character traits as reasons you love him, and write them down.

Samples:

> I love your verses with all my heart, dear Miss Barrett,—and this is no off-hand complimentary letter that I shall write,—whatever else, no prompt matter-of-course recognition of your genius and there a graceful and natural end of the thing: since the day last week when I first read your poems, I quite laugh to remember how I have been turning and turning again in my mind what I should be able to tell you of their effect upon me.
>
> —ROBERT BROWNING IN HIS FIRST LETTER TO HIS WIFE, ELIZABETH BARRETT BROWNING (BOTH POETS)[5]

> I already love in you your beauty, but I am only beginning to love in you that which is eternal and ever precious—your heart, your soul.
>
> —COUNT LEO TOLSTOY (AUTHOR) TO HIS FIANCÉE, VALERIA ARSENEV[6]

Thank God for your mate. Give thanksgiving to the Creator for the gift of your husband. In Philippians 1:3, the apostle Paul says, "I thank my God every time I remember you." Wouldn't it be nice to know that your husband does the same? Let your beloved know that he is one of the best blessings God ever gave you.

Samples:

> How full of joy & happiness the world seemed to me, for I felt that you are my own Nell—that you love me! I said, "I am content." I was happy and thanked God that he had so blessed me!
>
> —US PRESIDENT CHESTER ARTHUR TO HIS WIFE, ELLEN LEWIS HERNDON[7]

Each morning, as I rise,
I give thanks to God
For your presence
lying next to my bod.

—"Spock" to J on her birthday

Describe your love. Here are some final tips for describing your love.

Use nicknames if you have them. Winston Churchill (British prime minister) and his wife, Clementine, called each other "Pug" and "Cat" in their letters,[8] and the couple in Song of Songs called each other "Beloved."

Include analogies if you can think of any. Try it out in your head first by completing statements such as "Being with you is like ______" and "You are to me like ____ is to ____."

Stay away from clichés. "Roses are red, violets are blue" ain't gonna cut it, unless your next two lines are utterly brilliant. Also, his eyes may indeed "sparkle like the stars," but try to come up with something fresh.

Gush a little. Yes, it's okay to write stuff that would make your teenager want to vomit if he/she read it.

Keep it going. One love letter is awesome. Continuing this practice can be a great way to remind yourself why you love your husband and to be reminded why he loves you. The Brownings wrote 574 love letters to each other,[9] and Winston and Clementine Churchill wrote throughout their fifty-seven-year marriage. We need to hear now and then not only that we are loved but also why we are loved. Love letters are a great way to express that sentiment to your spouse.

"We've got fifteen minutes. Let's do this!"

That statement, or something like it, is said rather often in marriages, I fear. But far worse are those couples who seem to have *zero* minutes for sexual intimacy. How can husbands and wives find time to connect physically when the rest of life demands so much of our time?

All night long on my bed I looked
for the one my heart loves;
I looked for him but did not find him.

Song of Songs 3:1

Scheduling Sex

My best friend and I have a routine. We text back and forth about our calendars, find an open date, and schedule time to meet up for breakfast or lunch. Once a week or so, you can find us at a restaurant table for a social/work day. There are some predictable parts: We eat. We chat. We work on our laptops. But there's no agenda, no script. Sometimes we meet for an hour or two; other times we hunker down for maybe six hours of productivity. Sometimes we have serious discussions; sometimes we laugh ourselves so silly I wonder if others might be saying to the waitstaff, "I'll have what they're having."[10] Sometimes I'm good and get a salad; sometimes I get the juicy burger. *Always*, I enjoy our time together.

Why don't we treat sex in marriage this way? Of all the controversial topics about marital sexuality, scheduling sex continues to invite argument, with both advocates and opponents. For all those who swear scheduling sex has increased their marital intimacy, plenty reject the notion that scheduling sex is a good idea for their marriage. The naysayers are certain that putting sex on a schedule results in contrived, obligatory sex rather than passionate lovemaking.

But like lunch dates with my friend, there's no agenda, no script. Scheduling sex with your husband is merely prioritizing that activity enough to put it on your respective calendars. This can be especially important with spouses whose schedules rarely align or who juggle children's activities.

Once you get to your scheduled sex appointment, you can order whatever you want. You might have a quickie or hours-long lovemaking. You might stay in the bedroom or change up your location. You might go for the tried-and-true or spice it up with a new sexual activity or position. Spontaneity still exists in *what* you do together.

Try scheduling sex a few times, and see how it goes. It might feel forced at first, but so does that first lunch date with a friend. Once you get in a groove, you might find yourself happy with the results.

How to start. Many couples schedule once a week. They may get in other lovemaking sessions over those seven days, but most couples should be making love at least once a week. Ask your husband, "When are you free this week to have some *us time?*" Give a wink while saying "us time" and he might get the hint. Or you could come right out and say, "I want to carve out time for us to have sex this week. What day/evening is good for you?" Try not to make it like scheduling an office conference. Instead, view it like setting up a lunch date or a night out with a friend. Create anticipation of the experience as you describe your eagerness for time together.

How to show up. All that's required when scheduling sex is that you be willing to have sex at the time you committed to. If you have further expectations or desires for that time, express them when you arrive. If not, fall into each other's arms and see what happens. There's no agenda unless you make one. If you're among those who really desire spontaneity and struggle with this concept of scheduling, set the scene a little with music, candles, or whatever helps you get in the mood. Take deep breaths and remind yourself that this time is like any other hour in your day and you can make of it what you want.

How to evaluate. Don't make up your mind based on the first experience. The first time you do anything can be awkward, but you might come to love it within a short time. Show up a second and a third time and see if you two get into a groove—a Barry White kind of groove. Get a few times under your belt and then see how you both feel about it.

How to make it fun. Here are some ways couples have suggested for making scheduling sex more fun:

Buy a wall or desk calendar and mark those days with hearts or lips or some other sexy reminder. You could even introduce your own code. Write "YAM" for "you and me" time, or "RMW" for "rock my world." Be creative.

Build anticipation by flirting about the upcoming appointment.

Plant a big kiss on your honey in the morning before you go to work and say, "Plenty more of that coming tonight." Or text your husband, "Guess what I'm *not* wearing. You can see for yourself tonight. ;)" Find other ways to reference how you are looking forward to your special time.

Take turns planning other aspects of the event. One time hubby may choose the place and you choose the position, and then vice versa. Or each of you could have an opportunity to create the scene before the other arrives.

Make it a secret habit. If you both know that every Sunday afternoon after church you and your husband will be climbing the peak of pleasure, it can become your playful little secret.

Those nights of scheduled sex might become a happy tradition in your marriage. Give it a shot!

Unmatched Bedtimes

You may be married to a night owl who comes alive at the stroke of midnight. Or you might have a husband with an annoying habit of waking up early, throwing open the curtains, and greeting the morning by whistling songs at the highest possible decibels. (Can you tell which I am?) Very often, a night owl marries a morning person. As if you didn't have enough to work through with the family backgrounds and gender differences!

I chalk it up to another humorous part of marital sexuality—trying to get those schedules matched so that you can both enjoy some face-to-face, body-to-body time. Sometimes what gets in the way of getting it on is simply that you are exhausted by 11:00 p.m. and he's raring to go. Or you're up at the crack of dawn and have plenty of early-morning energy to make love while he's sprawled across the bed snoring and drooling into the pillow. What to do?

Perhaps you can benefit from my years of experience on what *doesn't* work:

Straddling his sleeping body and bouncing may arouse his little guy, but the big guy is still pretty dang tired and not so happy that he's awake.

Demanding in a hostile tone that he stay up later or wake up earlier is not likely to lead to a morning/evening of memorable lovemaking.

Trying to get the kids to bed earlier so you can enjoy time before one of you dozes off midsentence will work for one or two nights. Then the little knee-biters will consult their union manual and stage a rather effective protest.

What *does* work? Negotiation. And compromise. (Don't we married people *love* those words?)

Keeping similar bedtimes fosters opportunity for sexual intimacy in your marriage. Waking up together also encourages time together—for physical and emotional connection.

Maybe your compromise is that the night owl goes to bed early with the morning person, and after early bird falls asleep, night owl can get up again and stay awake as long as desired. Or you could negotiate some days of the week to go to bed early and other days to sleep in. Perhaps one of you shifts the schedule to match the other for now, knowing it can change in the future. (For instance, a stay-at-home mom might follow her husband's early-rising routine if she can manage a nap sometime in the day.) It's worth discussing your mismatched schedules to find a solution so you can spend more time together.

Too many couples have one spouse crawling into bed early while the other stays up watching television late into the night. In the morning, the early-to-bed one is indeed early to rise, and the night owl wakes long after. Before you know it, two people who vowed to love and cherish, be there for each other, and grow in intimacy pass each other daily like ships in the night. You lose your sense of emotional closeness, and the physical closeness fades as well. That's not the way it's meant to be.

Make it a priority to be in bed with your husband at times when you are both awake—morning or night. This will give you a chance to talk and cuddle together. And that will cultivate those moments of "Hey, while we're here ..." Then enjoy!

Drive-Through Sex: The Quickie

What is a *quickie*? According to Dictionary.com, it's "a hurried sexual encounter." A quickie can be any sexual experience—intercourse, oral sex, hand job, etc.—that occurs in a brief span of time. Personally, I would describe levels of sexual encounters with the following comparisons:

Extended lovemaking is like a five-star restaurant. Most of us don't go out to posh restaurants all the time. Those four-course meals that pamper our palates are a treat we enjoy on special occasions.

Usual sex is like a family restaurant. This is the place in our neighborhood where we know the menu, have a few favorites, and enjoy an hour or so of good dining. Nothing fancy, but definitely satisfying.

Quickies are like drive-throughs. Pick a fast-food place, get something to go, and eat quickly. Not recommended as a standard for meals but sates the hunger and can be yummy.

Just like passing through a McDonald's or Taco Bell drive-through, there are some things to remember when approaching the quickie.

Build anticipation before you pull into the drive-through.

It will be much easier to enjoy that quickie if you and hubby are flirting and doing small things for each other throughout the day. You won't have much time for foreplay before the quickie, so consider all of those things you do with and for each other outside the bedroom as foreplay. If you invest in your friendship, affection, and desire for each other, it can be a smoother transition to your hubby looking at you and saying, "Quick, let's have sex!" The quickie will become a brief physical expression of the longer experiences of deep love you've had outside the bedroom.

Make up your mind quickly. This ain't a white-tablecloth restaurant where the suited server will linger near your table for as long as you wish to peruse the menu before ordering. You drive up, glance at the menu choices, and lean close to the speaker to order. If you take twelve minutes to figure out what you want, you may end up with a traffic jam of angry drivers behind you honking their horns and yelling.

Likewise, if you and your husband want to have a quickie, decide fast what you'll do. Are you performing a hand job for him? Will you have intercourse? Is orgasm a must for you? Keep the expectations clear for what you're doing so you can both enjoy it for what it is. If you take twelve minutes to figure out what you want, you may end up with a traffic jam of needy children knocking at your door and yelling.

Speak clearly. Those drive-through speakers are not exactly high tech. If you want your order to arrive with some semblance of what you want, you'd better speak loudly and enunciate. You don't want the attendant hearing "pies" when you said "fries."

With the quickie, you must also speak clearly. This is no time to be patient while hubby slowly strokes the area around where you want to be touched until he finds the right spot ten minutes later. Speak up! Move his hand and say things like, "Right here feels good" or "That's the spot." Tell him if something hurts, feels good, or would be better another way. Communicate so he can get the order right.

Be prepared for grease. Despite the inclusion of salads on many fast-food menus, let's face it: most drive-through food is greasy. Everything is fried in oil, slathered in butter, or has a naturally high content of fat. You know that going in, so you aren't surprised when you bite into that battered chicken strip and juices seep out.

Bring out the grease with the quickie too! In other words, lubrication is key. Have your personal lubricant or coconut oil ready to go. If you're doing a hand job—which I've sometimes called a "lube job"—you'll probably need to add moisture. For intercourse, most wives take a substantial amount of time to become "wet" enough for penetration. You likely won't have time for that with a quickie, so get out the lubricant and slather it on.

Eat quickly. Um, yeah. Not going to describe this one. Use your imagination.

Leave satisfied. Admittedly, it's not the dining experience I'm going to write a magazine review about, but I like some drive-through food. It addresses my hunger. It fills my tummy. It hits the spot.

Similarly, the quickie should not be the go-to sexual encounter in marriage, but it has its place. There are times when longer intimate experiences are just not possible. You're at the in-laws' place, your children are young and need regular supervision, your work schedules don't match up. You wouldn't go without food simply because you don't have time to make it a three-course meal. Likewise, your marriage need not go without sex simply because time is currently in short supply. The quickie can sate your hunger and hit the spot.

Chapter 3
GETTING READY FOR SEX

Have you noticed that women in movies always seem ready for sex? As if that's been on their minds all day long? In reality, most wives spend their day navigating mundane tasks, like performing their day job, determining what to cook for dinner, and managing all that laundry.

Alas, sometimes you have to prepare your mind and body for sexual intimacy with your husband. So let's talk about lingerie, getting ready for an intimate encounter, and feeling comfortable naked with your man.

> Take me away with you—let us hurry!
>
> Song of Songs 1:4

How to Shop for Lingerie

Lingerie can include anything from a camisole and briefs to a long nightgown to a leather teddy. Whatever your idea of pretty, you can probably find something to wear to bed … and to let hubby remove. Lingerie can make you feel sexy and show you're making additional effort to appeal to your husband sexually.

Here are my tips for shopping for lingerie.

Fabrics. One of the standard complaints about alluring lingerie is that it's itchy or scratchy. Look for comfortable fabrics. Oftentimes, this means spending a little more, but not always. Cotton, silk, and satin will feel better than polyester, lace, and fake leather. If you want a lacy look, try something with the lace overlaid on a softer fabric.

Don't worry about checking labels or asking "What's this made of?" Just touch the fabric. Stroke a small section with your hands and ask whether you'd want that fabric rubbing against your more sensitive skin. Then buy what feels soft and sexy.

Body Type. What looks and feels good on a tall, thin woman isn't the same as what looks and feels good on a petite, buxom woman. Lingerie should play to your assets, while minimizing those areas that thrill you less.

Full-figured? Consider a babydoll, teddy, or two-piece design that is fitted around the bust and flares out toward the hemline. This will emphasize the bust but camouflage any extra inches around the torso. Remember that dark colors are slimming, so stay away from whites and pastels.

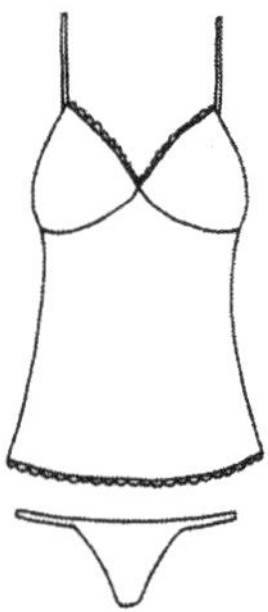

Tall and thin? A standard bra or camisole-and-panties combination flatters this figure. A garter belt will emphasize long legs.

Short and petite? Try a chemise or gown with a slit up the leg. This will make your legs appear longer, drawing the eye up toward the torso.

Athletic build? Boy shorts and "cheekies" emphasize muscular legs and a nice derriere. Pair them with a bra, camisole, or even a corset.

Bra/corset tips. Smaller busts look good in triangle bras or balconette styles. Average busts look good in demi (half-cup) and push-up styles. Larger busts look good with a full cup or plunge.

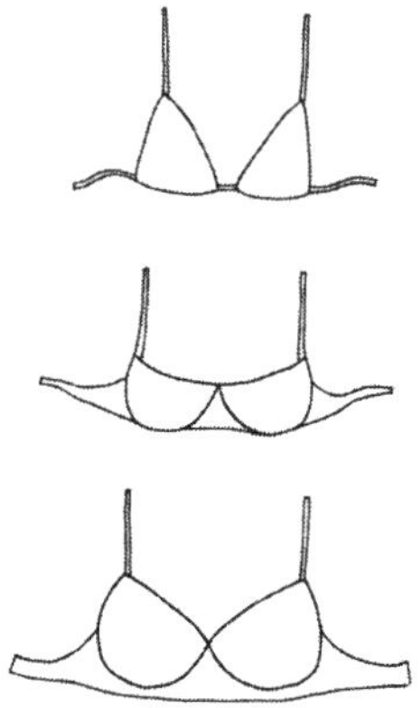

These guidelines aren't hard and fast, of course—just ideas to consider.

Your best bet is to enlist the help of a salesperson. She should be able to point out options for your shape and assets. Look through the store with an eye toward what will help you focus on your best attributes and feel confident.

Fit. Double-check your size. If you buy too small, you'll be uncomfortable and the garment won't hang well. If you buy too big, it won't show off your assets.

If it's been a while, get a bra fitting from a reputable store. Also, try on different sizes of lingerie in the dressing room. Remember that bras and undies should provide full coverage to look their best.

Comfort. A wife wants to feel confident about her body when she puts on lingerie. For some ladies, that means a black-and-red corset and a thong. For others, it means a silky nightgown with matching robe.

When buying lingerie both hubby and wife can enjoy, consider your comfort level. Get something that stretches you a little, but not too much. If you're in a sleep shirt most nights, you probably wouldn't feel comfortable donning nipple tassels and crotchless panties. Find something similar to what you already wear, but a little edgier, sexier, and more revealing.

For both of you. This lingerie experience is not solely for him. Sometimes men can communicate that message unwittingly (or wittingly). Most wives want to be appreciated, desired, beautiful ... but not ogled like a sixteen-ounce prime rib at the local steakhouse. You aren't being served on a platter. You're presenting your body in beautiful attire to appeal to your husband and to feel confident about the beauty God gave you. Look for lingerie that accomplishes that.

Why I Wear Lingerie, Though Hubby Doesn't Care

In my own many years of marriage, I've learned my husband doesn't care about lingerie. *Really*. Doesn't care.

This is atypical. A majority of husbands delight in seeing their wives don pretty, suggestive attire in the bedroom. For those women, I encourage you to find something you're willing to wear to bed that will also arouse his senses.

But even if your husband is fine with bypassing the nightie and going straight to nude, maybe you should invest in a few pieces of beautiful lingerie for yourself. Why? Here are a few reasons:

It focuses your mind. Much of a woman's sex drive is in her head. In a single moment, we gals entertain an average of 342 things in our brains (give or take a couple), and shoving out all that extraneous stuff to focus on making love can be a mental battle some days. So how can you shift from being super-mommy, super-worker, super-cook, super-house-manager, etc. and become super-sexy-wife?

Slipping on lingerie can get you in the right frame of mind. You commit to that focus of being physical with your husband. After all, once you put on a lace teddy, you're probably not thinking about cleaning the toilets anymore. The rest of your to-do list can wait.

It makes you feel sexy. A good piece of lingerie will play to your body's figure and show off your physical assets. It will help you display your best features in an enticing way. Lingerie usually has a softer texture and lighter fabric, and that satin or lace or silk can brush your skin in a pleasant way. All that comes together to remind you that you are one sexy lady.

Just try to get that same feeling wearing an oversized tee and granny panties. Not gonna happen. There's something about lingerie—lingerie you like—that makes you feel desirable.

It sends a clear signal. When you walk into your bedroom wearing provocative lingerie, there's no need to say to your husband, "Hey, you wanna?" You're sending a pretty clear signal—no words necessary.

This approach can make some guys practically giddy—particularly those husbands whose wives rarely initiate. If you show up looking interested and inviting, it's like his birthday wish came true. And now he gets to unwrap the present. (Best. Birthday. Ever.)

If you get mixed messages in your marriage like "I was interested, but you looked busy" or "Well, I would have, but I thought you had to get up early" or "I didn't know if you were kissing me good night or kissing me to initiate something," then sending a clear signal can be a welcome event. Wearing pretty lingerie and presenting yourself as one hot wife can tell your hubby he's one lucky, lucky man. And he'd better use this opportunity well.

What if he truly doesn't care about lingerie? Maybe, like my husband, he prefers the clear signal of showing up naked. Or perhaps sexy lingerie really doesn't have an arousing effect on him.

Or maybe your husband's low sex drive includes him not caring about lingerie. If slipping on something sexy and posing in your bedroom doorway results in little more than a passing nod from your hubby, should you stick to the tattered tee and pajama pants?

Clearly, a major mismatch in sexual drives is a bigger issue than what you wear to bed. But while you're working on that, I suggest you buy some pretty stuff for you. Maybe you're not going to get a rise from your husband by wearing it, at least not until you've figured out what his obstacles are and have dealt with them. However, you may need some personal reminders from time to time that you are beautiful and sexy and worthwhile. You want to feel pretty for yourself, even if that nightie stays on you all night long.

Prepping for Sex

You are planning to have sex soon. Or he is hoping for it. But right now, you're in that take-it-or-leave-it mood. Or maybe even a leave-it-or-leave-it mood. Sigh.

If you waited to be perfectly "in the mood" every single time, your marriage might not experience another sexual encounter for months. Or you could get lucky this weekend. But you're supposed to be having sex tonight.

Instead of waiting to get hit by the lightning bolt of lovemaking, you can create some electricity yourself. You can get yourself in the mood.

Here are some tips on how to prepare yourself for sex. Try one or more and see what works for you.

Build anticipation. We tend to enjoy what we anticipate. Got a vacation coming up? A birthday? A massage? We think ahead about what that will be like and plan how much we will enjoy its arrival. Try doing the same thing with sexual intimacy in your marriage. Think ahead about when you'll make love later.

If you're planning a night of hot-and-heavy, let images come to mind throughout the day. Think about the attractiveness of your husband, the way you felt the last time he kissed you or when you last climaxed, the joy of becoming physically one flesh, and God's gift of sex. Pray your evening will go well, and that you'll both find pleasure and connection with each other. As you let the anticipation build, your body may respond with more readiness when the moment arrives.

Remove distraction. One of the greatest difficulties for wives is distraction. Female brains are typically able to juggle more balls than a Las Vegas act. We have so much else going on in our lives and around our houses that asking us to focus on sex is like asking that juggler to toss a single ball. We get antsy.

But you won't be able to relax and enjoy the pleasure of sex with your husband unless you focus. Do your best to remove distractions. Get the kids to bed early. Straighten up the bedroom. Put away your to-do list. Do whatever you need to do to put down those balls and get into The Act.

Prepare the location. Atmosphere matters. We instinctively know this when we enter restaurants and get an immediate feel for the food based on the surroundings. Likewise, we can create a mood by preparing the location of our lovemaking. That might mean taking the time to refurbish your bedroom to make it a pleasant place, adding ambiance enhancers like candlelight and music, or creating an inviting space for the two of you to feel as excited as a pair of mating-season rabbits. It could even be as simple as getting the LEGO blocks and the Barbie dolls out of your bedroom.

Consider what environment would evoke your romantic and sexy side. Then make the effort to have your bedroom reflect that environment.

Awaken sensation. We have five senses: sight, smell, hearing, touch, and taste. Sexual intimacy is particularly focused on sight and touch but can involve all five senses. To get in the mood, try to awaken those other senses. Light a scented candle and inhale deeply. Turn on a sexual intimacy playlist and close your eyes to listen. Take a bubble bath and feel the hot water and foam stroke your skin. Replace your regular sheets with satin ones. Bring chocolate-covered strawberries or champagne into the bedroom.

Think of things that are not specifically sexual but *sensual*. Find ways to awaken your senses so you'll be ready when your senses are engaged in lovemaking.

Ask for affection. Wives often need more affectionate foreplay before feeling ready to make love. Let's be honest, ladies: holding off a horny husband from going straight to the erogenous zones can be like defending your kingdom with a Nerf sword. At some point, you want to yell, "Hey! Hold hands first, handle hooha later!"

Yet one of the sexiest things ever is your husband stroking you gently with his broad, manly hands. Or that soft-lipped, melting-into-each-other kiss that lingers until the tingle runs all the way down to your pinkie toes. Ask for the affection you need. Explain that you might get in the mood if you spent some time touching, kissing, snuggling, or getting a massage. Ten to fifteen minutes of that, and you might be eager to make love even if you weren't before.

Use communication. Most husbands love to turn their wives on. But no husband can read his wife's mind.

Tell your hubby what feels good. You can use words, moans, or shrieks, but communicate clearly what you enjoy in the bedroom. It can feel awkward at first to say things like "Over here is better" or "I love it when you ___." But the initial discomfort passes, and most husbands are receptive to positively phrased suggestions.

Pay attention. Whatever preparation you've done before, you still need to pay attention to what's happening in the moment. Once you come together with your husband, think about what's happening to your body and to his. You can open your eyes and watch your bodies melding or gaze at his facial expressions. Or you can close your eyes and focus on the nerves of your skin as they awaken with his touch. Hone in on your erogenous zones and focus your mental energy on their arousal.

If your mind wanders, bring it back to the moment at hand. You might need to do this a few times before your mind is fully engaged. But do your best to give that time of sexual intimacy your full, undivided attention.

If you use these tips to prepare yourself for sex, you might find yourself more in the mood for lovemaking than you originally felt. Hopefully, you can get turned on as you progress into this sexual encounter with your husband.

Getting Comfortable Being Naked with Your Husband

Dim the bedroom lights. Cue the burlesque jazz music. Step into the bedroom wearing nothing but a smile. What do you get?

Well, you either get a happy hubby, a super self-conscious wife, or more likely both.

How can wives disrobe and display their goods to their husbands with confidence? How do you reach the point where you can enter your bedroom, where hubby awaits, with simply a smile and a swagger? Here are some thoughts on sorting through our self-doubts.

He wants to see you naked. Whether you understand it or not, God has infused your husband with an appreciation of feminine beauty and especially nudity. Specifically, your nudity. You don't have to look like a supermodel. You are beautiful because you are *all woman*—which is entirely different from him and therefore incredibly intriguing and arousing.

You have curves. You have breasts. You have soft flesh. You have tender, exciting places. Whether you also have ten extra pounds and some varicose veins doesn't detract from all the goodies he sees. We wives need to recognize that God created men to be visually excitable creatures, and your hubby is aroused by and interested in your naked body. So show it off!

It's the only body you have. You can spend your whole life wishing you were taller, shorter, curvier, thinner, fuller, flatter, lighter, darker, etc. But this is the body you have. And it's a pretty good one. Hasn't it served you well in many ways?

Plenty of people with unusual challenges like paraplegia or malnutrition or terminal illness would love to have the very body someone else complains about all day long. I'm not trying to give you what-for just because you're unhappy with some aspect of your body. That's understandable. We all have something we might want to change, and the feelings that come with that simply are. But learning to appreciate what you have goes a long way toward being willing to share it with your husband.

Since this is your body, find ways to love it. Keep it healthy. Enhance what you can. Focus on your best features. Live in gratitude for your body. Get over thinking you want someone else's, and intentionally learn to appreciate the body you have.

Remember, he ain't perfect either. I find my husband very attractive, even though I objectively realize he will not be named *People*'s Sexiest Man Alive any time soon. He's my flavor of man, so I think he's "the bomb." Why not believe your hubby feels the same way about you?

He loves you, and that impacts how he sees you—making your beauty shine and your flaws seem insignificant. Moreover, he recognizes that you're both aging, that wrinkles and gravity are taking their slow toll, and he doesn't expect you to look like a twenty-year-old for the rest of your life. (Some of us didn't look our best at twenty anyway!) He knows you aren't perfect, but he isn't perfect either. You can still be perfect for each other.

You've been through so much together, what's a little peep show? Honestly, this one has contributed a lot to my level of comfort around my husband. What's the big deal about showing him my body after all we've been through together?

We've experienced the better and the worse, the richer and the poorer, the sickness and the health. We've seen each other at our strongest of times and our most vulnerable. We've nursed each other through stomach flu, surgeries, and grief. We are intimately connected in every other way, so why would I withhold this one way?

If you want that deep connection with your husband, you have to open yourself up. You need to trust him with your heart and with your body. You aren't likely to have a fabulous marriage in every other aspect if you cannot be vulnerable and open in the marriage bed. Chalk it up to one more thing that makes your relationship unique. You walk through life together in a way you don't with anyone else, including the way you share your bodies with each other.

Find out what's keeping you from sharing all your naked glory with your husband and then address it. Your sexual intimacy will be even more intimate when you become comfortable about being nude with him.

Tips for Confidently Baring It All for Your Hubby

You're convinced you need to let your husband see and appreciate your body. But how can you grow more comfortable and confident baring it all for your hubby? (Because yeah, he wants you to. He told me so.)

Here are specific tips for getting over your trepidation and sharing your body more freely with your husband.

Focus on what you like about your body. We all have especially good features and less appealing "flaws." (Although "flaws" isn't the right word.) We ladies tend to focus on what we believe is wrong with our bodies. Perhaps we think that attitude keeps us humble, but it's not boasting to recognize your best features and revel in how God made you. You are "wonderfully made" (Psalm 139:14).

So take stock, girlfriend! Check. You. Out. Stand in front of a full-length mirror, consider compliments you've received, figure out what you like about your fabulous body. Be specific. For instance, my list would include the texture of my hair, the dimple that appears on one cheek when I smile super-big, the color of my eyes, and my navel (we all have a preference for outty or inny, and I happen to like what I got).

Then look for ways to display those features to your husband. And rehearse the list in your head when you disrobe. You'll feel better knowing what unique and beautiful traits you have to offer for your husband's viewing pleasure.

Stop comparing. Don't compare your body to someone else's or to the body you had once upon a time (or could have if Spanx made a beneath-the-flesh product). This is tough because advertisers are on a near-rampage to have you feel "less than" so you'll buy their products to feel "as good as." "Want to look as good as [insert hot celebrity's name here]? Buy our [diet pill, home gym, clothing, plastic surgery, etc.]!" Don't get sucked into comparison games.

And don't wait for perfection before you bare your body. Your husband's probably not comparing you to anyone else. I hear from hubbies all the time who essentially say about their wives, "You are altogether beautiful, my darling; there is no flaw in you" (Song of Songs 4:7). Are their wives objectively perfect? I doubt it. But they believe it.

Stop holding yourself to an impossible standard. The only real standard is who you are, the best you can be today, and your husband's affirmation.

But the even better, higher, truer standard is God Himself—how He sees you. God doesn't lie, and He thinks you're amazing. Beautiful. Stunning.

Take care of your body. I'm going to be frank with you here, girlfriend. I know why some wives aren't confident baring it all: we've let our bodies go. We used to eat better, exercise more, dress nicer, style our hair, get out of pajamas at least once during the day. Whether you've acted clueless about your transformation from beauty to beast (no, it's not that bad), or you beat yourself up so much you're craving another pint of Ben & Jerry's to feel better, you know who you are.

I don't want to add another straw of shame to the camel's back. By no means! I'm on your side. As a writer, I work from home, with my laptop as my constant companion. So it's ever-so-tempting to have my entire wardrobe be yoga pants and oversized T-shirts. My hair adores quick-and-dirty ponytails. I haven't been to my exercise class in ... no idea. And believe me, something happens after age forty! Suddenly lettuce leaves seem to add as much to my waistline as a dish of chocolate mousse. Yes, it's an ongoing challenge.

But when we attend to our health and grooming, we look and feel better. Moreover, the Bible encourages good health with warnings against gluttony (actually calling it sin!). Scripture says our bodies are "temples of the Holy Spirit" (1 Corinthians 6:19), and Proverbs 31 gives the example of the well-clothed and hard-working wife. So let's take care of ourselves, for heaven's sake!

Don't sweat the number on the scale or go in search of some unrealistic, useless beauty ideal (see point above). Simply get healthy and be the best possible you! You'll feel better about the body you have to bare for your husband.

Prepare for the unveiling. So you're still nervous about getting naked, huh? Totally understandable. With the exception of that junior high communal dressing room for physical education [insert bad memories here], you don't generally get naked in front of other people. Your nude body is none of anyone's business. Except it's your husband's business. Your body belongs to him too (1 Corinthians 7:4).

How can you calm your nerves and put your best foot (body) forward? Prepare. Take a bubble bath. Set the scene with special lighting, like candlelight or a low lamp. Choose lingerie that highlights your assets. Turn on calming or intimate music. Take

Lamaze-type breaths. Use meditation techniques. Go to your "happy place."

This isn't the time to Go Big or Go Home—more like Go Slow. Take your time, breathe deeply, and take it easy. *You can do this*. Like anything else you fear, it gets easier the second time and the third time and the fourth time. It will get better—but only if you take that first step.

Consider his reaction. When wives bare it all, most husbands look like they've just opened their favorite Christmas present. "For me? It's *exactly* what I wanted!" We women can get so caught up in thinking about how we look or staring at our "problem areas," we don't attend to hubby's reactions. Which could be just the reassurance we need.

If you can't tell what he likes by facial expressions, ask! Many guys don't think to enumerate what they find so appealing. Look, I'm married to a guy who seems to think words are on a rationing list somewhere. If I need to hear something specific, I've learned to ask. Once I throw out the question—like "What are your favorite parts of my body and why?"—he'll answer with a list resembling the husband in Song of Songs.

Then believe your husband. If he says your breasts are "like clusters of fruit" (a compliment. Really. Check out Song of Songs 7:7), accept it! Tell yourself again and again and again that it's true. He really thinks you're sexy.

Be confident. Feel beautiful. Bare it all for your hubby.

Chapter 4
KISSING

Ah, the kiss! That brilliant invention of our Creator that makes us check our breath, tilt our heads, plant a big wet one, and hunger for more. Plenty of Christians writing about sex believe the orgasm is proof our Creator designed mating for pleasure. While I agree, the kiss is an excellent example as well. After all, kisses are not required for reproduction, so what's their point?

Puh-leasure, people! So pucker up and let's talk about kissing.

> Let him kiss me with the kisses of his mouth.
>
> SONG OF SOLOMON 1:2

Types of Kisses

Kisses have been lauded for a long time as a beautiful expression of love between a man and a woman. Yet sometimes we forget to keep the romance alive through tender and passionate kissing in our marriages.

In 1955, French actress Jeanne Bourgeois said, "A kiss can be a comma, a question mark, or an exclamation point."[11] How true! The type of kiss can say a lot about what is going on between the two kissers. And—like grammar—there is room for all kinds of punctuation.

Now, there are several types of kisses—from the quick peck to the soft exploring kiss to the open-mouthed twisting of tongues. And they all have their place.

Butterfly Kiss. This kiss is often given from parent to child and vice versa. It involves blinking one's eyes to rub eyelashes against another's cheek or some other area of skin. It's sweet, but not particularly romantic. If you get hot and bothered from a butterfly kiss from your husband, it's been way too long since you had some nookie.

Peck. Pecks are those quick puckered-up kisses usually given in a hurry as one of you rushes out the door. A peck can also be a nice way of kissing in public without making everyone cover their eyes or puke. Pecks are great for what they are—a quick reminder that you love this man and cherish him.

Face Kiss. This is when one of you kisses the other anywhere on the face—cheek, forehead, nose, etc. A face kiss allows one of you to express affection or distract your spouse from whatever he/she is doing. Like if I'm writing on my laptop, and my husband starts kissing my forehead, my check, my chin ... *Wait, where was I?* Anyway, you get the idea. Soft kisses on the face are initiated by one partner but usually appreciated by the other.

Soft Lip Kiss. My favorite! A soft lip kiss is leaning in and tenderly kissing your spouse's lips. Lips are parted like a cracked door or a hot dog bun—a small opening, not too much. This soft kiss should last several seconds, lingering on one another's delicious lips. It can be enjoyed by itself or as a teaser for a more passionate kiss. Many classic Hollywood kisses are soft lip kisses and leave us wanting more.

French Kiss. I don't know why the French get credit for

this one. Were they the only ones with tongues? I think not. It's also called "tongue hockey" (lovely, eh?). Basically, you tangle tongues and share saliva. A great French kiss is incredibly passionate and can tickle you all the way to your toes. A terrible French kiss chokes you or leaves you calling the HazMat team to clean up all the extra spit. The best French kiss is gentle and flexible. Don't attack your husband's mouth; tease, explore, and enjoy it.

Licking Kiss. A licking kiss involves your tongue stroking his tongue, teeth, lips, etc. This can be a titillating move, as long as you remember this is your honey's mouth and not the Tootsie Roll lollipop you must reach the center of. Take it slow, and use your tongue lightly.

Nibbling Kiss. How much should you involve your teeth in the process of kissing? Some people like to nibble on their spouse's lips. Notice I said "nibble," not "bite." Yes, vampires are all the rage, but if you feel a fangs-in impulse with your beloved, that's not cool. Stick to a nice, soft use of your teeth. Of course, some people don't like this at all, so gauge your husband's pleasure as you try it.

I've described kissing types in reference to the lips, but you can pucker up, lick, and nibble almost anywhere on your husband's body (as long as he enjoys it too).

Here are a few questions to ask him:

What is your favorite type of kiss?
How important is kissing to your feeling loved and cherished?
How can I be a better kisser?
Do you want to kiss right now?

Hopefully, that's the last question you'll get in before your lips and tongues entangle. It might lead to other things, or if your house is like mine, it might lead to your kids walking in and saying, "Eeewww!" Either way, it's a better use of a few seconds than whatever else you were going to do.

Tips for Kissing

Before you first jumped into bed with your honey, I bet you tasted his lips, and something there made you want to come back. Once you got married, however, some of that luscious lip locking probably fell by the wayside, and now you need a refresher course.

Here are a few tips for fantastic, fun-filled, fabulous, frisky, frenzied kissing.

Your breath. It matters. But you are the last person to know whether you're experiencing a bout of halitosis. It's funny how we breathe onto our palms, sniff them, and expect that to tell us something. Do you smell your own sweat when you've been excessively exercising? Do your kids recognize when they have foot odor? No. Your breath will just smell like your breath to you, unless you make it smell minty or yummy. Toothpaste, mints, mouthwash—these are our friends. Use them. Especially if you recently ate something with a strong taste or aroma.

Lips. Loose lips sink ships and communicate, "I can't be bothered to pucker." Tight lips indicate a controlling personality or anxiety. Relax your lips, but shape them so they can be easily kissed.

Tongue. My worst kisser—a former date from long ago—had a twelve-foot tongue. Okay, maybe not. But he used it like a boa constrictor invading my mouth. If you're not sure how to use your tongue in an open-mouthed kiss, think of the word *tease*. Tease your husband with your tongue. When full passion arrives, you can twist your tongues together to your heart's delight, but your tongue still shouldn't fill his entire mouth.

Hands. Where you place your hands is important. Kissing without touching can feel impersonal, yet immediately grabbing bums or private parts when going in for the smooch is not romantic. As your lips caress his, your hands should caress as well. You can caress shoulders, arms, back, hair, and face. You can also use your hands to draw your partner in or gently position him at a better angle.

Eyes. Open or closed? I'm not a stickler on this one. Some people think it's weird to be watched at such a close distance while being kissed, so they prefer closed. For others, visual stimuli helps them concentrate on the sensation of the kiss.

You can enjoy kissing for its own beauty, or it can lead to something else. I wish I could do a quick survey and ask wives if they feel their husbands kiss them often enough without expecting further sexual activity. My prediction would be that many wives would say no.

If you doubt the wonderful gift of kissing from God, try it out for a while in your marriage. Jim Burns of the *HomeWord* radio show suggests married couples have a fifteen-second kiss every day. Returning to the courtship of kissing might have a glorious effect on many couples.

When His Kiss Tastes Bad

One of my blog readers asked for tips on dealing with her husband, who chewed tobacco. She loved to kiss, but his habit was a big turn-off.

Before I married, I dated one guy who dipped and one guy who smoked. While they didn't do it right before we kissed, those habits don't exactly scream, "Put your mouth on mine!" In fact, I've often wondered where we even came up with such ideas.

Who was the first person to stick a bunch of leaves in a piece of paper, roll it up, and light it inches from his mouth? Who first grabbed a wad of tobacco leaves and shoved it between his lip and teeth to gnaw on for a while?

Other substances in one's mouth can also make for a less-than-approachable set of lips—like foods with pungent flavors and alcohol. While you might wish your honey would stop using or eating whatever is turning you off, don't hold your breath. Especially when it comes to tobacco. That's hard to quit. It can be done, and I hope your husband will make healthy choices for himself and for you. But it is a struggle, and he may not quit. Yet you still want to smooch with your mate.

There seem to be two issues here: what's actually going on with his mouth, and how you think and feel about it. Thus, you have a few options.

Talk to him. Tell your hubby you love to kiss him and want to do so freely, but you are bothered by his habit. Ask that he brush his teeth, use a mouthwash, chew a fresh-breath gum, or suck on a mint before you two kiss. You might even come up with a cute way to remind him in the moment. Let's say he leans in for a smackeroo, and you ask, "Are you lickable?" or "Minty mouth or tobacco tongue?" Discuss in advance what kind of freshen-up-to-kiss reminders he'd prefer.

Vary your kisses. If you think your hubby's been chewing or smoking or eating something that makes you queasy, keep your kisses closed-mouth. Or kiss other places on him. When you know his mouth is fresh, move in for the make-out. Don't be stingy with the kisses, but give clues as to when you are more interested in open-mouth kissing. He might notice the pattern and ask what's going on, or you can explain. Hopefully, he'll understand that you do desire to put your mouth on his, but you feel more comfortable doing so when his mouth is clean.

Use a demonstration. This one depends on your husband's sense of humor. So read him carefully and proceed cautiously. But you might pick a substance he hates and eat it in front of him. Then move in for a kiss and watch his reaction. If he flinches, you can laugh and say something like, "What? You don't want a garlic kiss?" If you two laugh about it, explain that you feel the same way about the befouling substance he uses. (I could easily make this point in my house by devouring tuna fish and going in for the kill. And my hubby knows better than to kiss me after eating peanut butter. I'd jump away from his lips like a wild hokey-pokey move.) Hopefully your husband will understand your point and approach kissing with a fresh mouth.

Get over it. All that said, it won't hurt you to kiss someone who has been chewing, smoking, drinking, eating onions, etc. You can retrain your mind to focus on the physical sensations of the kiss. It will take time to move your thoughts away from "gross" to "great." But our brains are pretty powerful, and we can master our thought processes by practicing. If you want to try, simply use this approach when you begin to kiss: Every time your mind turns to the yuck factor, refocus on how his tongue is touching yours, or the feel of his hand on your back, or the texture of his hair as you run your hand through it. Get the idea? Over time, your mind will readjust, and you'll be able to think about the kiss more than the taste-bud-killer that was there an hour ago.

And when your dear hubby does present himself all fresh and kissable, make it worth his while.

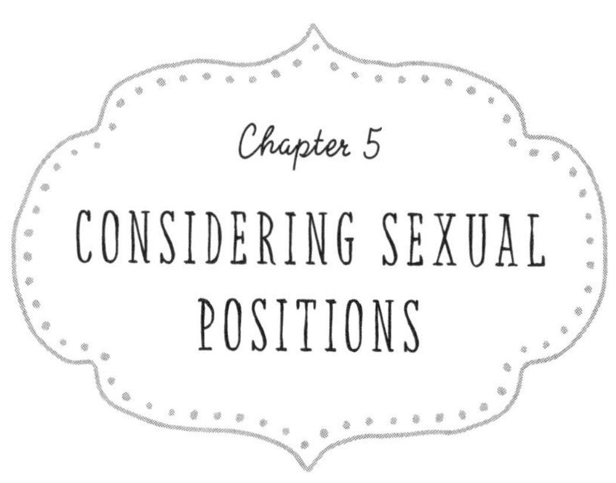

Chapter 5
CONSIDERING SEXUAL POSITIONS

With my odd sense of humor, I am ever so tempted to use the following quote for this section's intro: "Take your positions" (Jeremiah 46:4). But since the next part is "Put on your helmets, sharpen your spears, and prepare your armor," that's probably not the right choice.

Still, many believe there is a reference to sexual positioning in the Bible, where the Song of Songs wife twice refers to the way her husband holds her. And it doesn't sound like the "missionary position."

> His left arm is under my head
> and his right arm embraces me.
>
> Song of Songs 2:6 and 8:3

The Mission for a New Position

I was in the public library once and happened upon the marriage help section. Seeing a title on marital sexuality written by a couple of Christian authors I recognized, I picked up the book and thumbed through. Turning to the chapter on positions, I expected to find delicious secrets of sexual positioning, a treasure trove of interesting approaches, a veritable awakening of information regarding the many ways a husband and wife can connect in lovemaking.

There were four positions—described very dryly—all of which my husband and I had done within our first two weeks as newlyweds. Hardly the revelation I was expecting. When I mentioned this to a friend, she remarked that three of those positions would be news to some couples.

Since Christian authors have generally had little to say about positions, many Christian couples turn to the Kama Sutra instead. The Kama Sutra is an ancient Indian Hindu text that includes advice about sexual pleasure and has a chapter on positions for coitus. Sixty-four positions are described.

The Bible's definitive text on godly sexuality does not specifically describe sexual positions for married couples. However, scholars contend that there are clues to positions used by the Lover and the Beloved (the husband and wife in Song of Songs).

So should a Christian couple pursue different positions? Should they consult secular resources? What about those sixty-four positions in the Kama Sutra? How many of those are worthwhile?

I've looked at books and websites and had conversations with some very close friends.* And my hubby and I have tried some of the positions I've found. Based on research and experimentation, let me share what I've discovered.

There are only a few main positions, but many variations.

---

* I don't consult secular sources that use photographs as instructional material, since using a resource that has paid two people to pose in sexual positions for an audience is not God-honoring in my book. I don't get sex ideas from hard porn or soft porn.

Those sixty-four positions in the Kama Sutra, and any others people come up with, are really variations within a few major categories. The missionary position (lying down, man on top, woman on bottom, face-to-face) is probably the most obvious category. But how that feels for both partners can vary depending on where you place your legs, feet, arms, etc. Rear entry is another category. But how much you bend your body and where you place your hands provides different sensations.

Some positions are unrealistic. I agree completely with an excellent blog post from Julie Sibert of Intimacy in Marriage titled "Hey, I'm a Housewife, Not a Gymnast."[12] Some positions require a contortionist to perform … or a willingness to undergo traction later. And for the husband, let's just say that some things don't bend the way certain pictures indicate. If any man can do the position I once saw in a diagram, in which the hubby is in a full back bend, he should try out for the Olympic gymnastics team or Cirque du Soleil. That one is definitely not happening for most couples.

Varying positions provides several benefits. Here are some examples:

Visual stimulation. Watching yourself and your spouse connect from different perspectives can be titillating. For example, woman-on-top may be particularly appealing for a husband to view his wife's beautiful body.

Access. Certain positions provide better access to body parts you want to touch or kiss. For example, a wife may wish to stroke her husband's testicles by sitting atop him, or the husband could enter from the rear to more easily fondle his wife's breasts.

Control. You may want to vary who has more control over the time of entry, thrusting, and pacing. At times, the wife might wish to have more say for when she is ready for penetration—and that may be easier for her to do from above. Other times, the husband may want to take charge.

Sensation. The husband penetrating his wife from different angles provides different sensations. For instance, rear entry may be more comfortable for wives with a retroverted uterus. Also, certain positions have a greater chance of engaging the ever-elusive G-spot (though some couples never find it and enjoy sex just fine).

It's okay to be adventurous, and it's okay to not be adventurous. Not every position is worth trying, and positioning alone is not the secret to having a great sex life. Spending your time developing a loving, intimate relationship with your husband is much more worthwhile than reading through the Kama Sutra or any other sex manual. Don't go making a list of all sixty-four positions with a box to check off beside each one.

The best way to start is to vary your regular position(s) a little. Move your arms or legs somewhere else. Tilt slightly to the left or right. Angle yourselves a bit differently. Involve a chair or the side of the bed to create slightly different positioning.

This isn't about trying everything so you can say you've done it all. It's one key to a great sex life with your husband—loving him enough to find ways for both of you to experience physical pleasure. If changing up your positioning increases your enjoyment of each other, go for it! If you're both ecstatic with that one perfect position you've got going, keep at it. If your husband wants to try something new and you're reluctant, give it a chance. You might end up enjoying it after all.

Trying Positions

Let's say you're convinced that you want to add one, two, or twelve sexual positions to your marriage bed repertoire. Where do you start? Besides a back bend (heaven help us all), what are the options?

Sexual positions are derived from various ways to maneuver your bodies. Here are the main categories with a few variations on each theme.

Relative positioning

Man on top, face-to-face.
Woman on top, face-to-face.
Side by side, facing each other.
Rear entry, husband entering wife's vagina from behind.

General positioning

Husband and wife are lying down—mostly, at least.
One or both of you kneel on your knees.
The wife sits on her husband's lap.
Both husband and wife are standing.

Torso and limbs angling

Crouched. Your knees are bent, and your torso leans forward. For a wife, this creates a shorter distance between entry and the end of her vagina. Bending in this way can increase the likelihood of her husband thrusting into her elusive G-spot.

Spread wide. The wife spreads her legs wide, which gives the best access for viewing, touch, and entry. In this position, the husband may be able to go deeper into her vagina as well.

Legs together. When a wife keeps her legs together, it tightens the opening a bit, providing the man's penis and the woman's entry greater friction.

Legs bent. The wife can bend one or both legs slightly, moderately, or all the way up to her chest. Each configuration provides a different sensation to both the husband and the wife. For instance, the knees-to-chest position can feel more intense and allow the penis to brush against the wife's G-spot.

Legs up. Lifting the legs changes the angle of the body. Throwing your legs in the air may feel awkward at first, but trust me that it has its benefits. A wife can even drape her legs over her husband's shoulders.

Mix and Match. You can come up with all kinds of positions by mixing and matching. Let me show you what I mean.

Here's your typical sexual position: man on top, lying down, legs bent.

And here's the variation: man on top, standing, wife's legs up.

How about woman on top, sitting, legs bent?

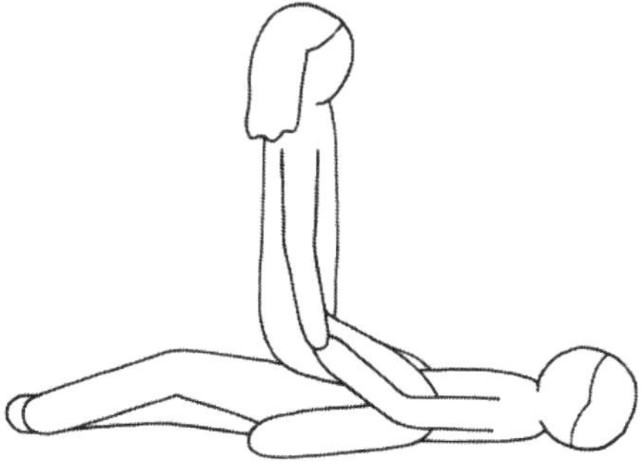

Or rear entry, kneeling, wife's legs together.

See what I mean? You can achieve numerous positions just with these basics.

Also, the wife tilting her hips is another way to shift the angle and feel something different. For example, in that last position, the wife can move her chest toward the bed or ground and tilt her hips up to meet her husband. In the missionary position, she can tilt her hips up off the bed.

If you've never tried anything adventurous in this area, start small. Keep two positions the same as usual and change the third. For example, use the same direction and position but change the angle. Or keep direction and angle but change general position. You get the idea.

Song of Songs 2:6 says, "His left arm is under my head, and his right arm embraces me." That certainly doesn't appear to be the missionary position. It sounds like side by side to me. I guess the Lover and the Beloved were a little adventurous themselves.

Why Try More than One Sexual Position

When you choose a position, there's no rule that you must follow through with it from kickoff to climax. Why not try more than one position in a single sexual encounter?

Remember that a sexual position is made up of several categories, like general positioning, relative positioning, and angling of your torso and limbs. Changing positions can involve something simple like flipping direction or raising your legs. Or it can be a totally new alignment. More than one position within an encounter can increase both your pleasure and your intimacy. For instance, making love can feel more intimate face-to-face, eye-to-eye, but rear entry might give you a stronger climax. So why not do both? Face each other for a while and enjoy that connection, then shift into the more physically arousing position.

Each of you will respond better to some positions than others—and you may not have the same favorites. Perhaps you can make love in the way that helps you reach climax—including the opportunity for your husband to manually stimulate you during intercourse, if needed—and then switch to what works best for him. Then both of you get what turns you on most.

Be willing to explore and experiment, and then analyze each position together. What does it feel like when we do X? How about Y? How do X and Y compare to Z? With all the results lined up, it's fairly easy to sort out what you do and don't like. This is especially nice to try when you have enough time to sample and savor the experience—when orgasm isn't on-the-clock, so to speak. (You parents with young'uns know what I'm talking about!)

If you're making minor adjustments in your positioning, you can likely accomplish that without any fanfare. Just move your legs, hips, whatever, and get the new angle going. But if you're going to make a big change in sexual positioning midway through, you must communicate that. Your communication need not be verbal, but you have to be able to coordinate what's happening next.

You can talk out beforehand which positions you're going to try, and then signal when it's time to switch to the next one. Or you can talk it through as you make love (e.g., "I want to get on top," or "Can you flip over?"). Alternatively, you can let your hands do the talking. Point in the direction you want to go, or move your partner's body to the position you desire.

Including several positions in your sexual intimacy repertoire can enhance the experience, physically and emotionally, for both of you. But remember, this ain't the Olympics. You don't get extra points for doing the triple Axel jump or a reverse somersault dive in the middle of lovemaking. You don't have to break the bed or your hip joints to enjoy some change-ups in sexual positioning.

Take it easy on yourself and start by shifting a bit here and there. If you're more adventurous (and younger than I am), you can try those positions that make some people tilt their heads and ask, *How do they do that?* But the point of sex with your mate is not to brag that you've run the gamut of possibilities or won the Most Sexual Positions Tried trophy. It's about intimacy and pleasure. If changing up your sexual positions accomplishes that, go for it. If a position doesn't enhance your lovemaking, leave it behind.

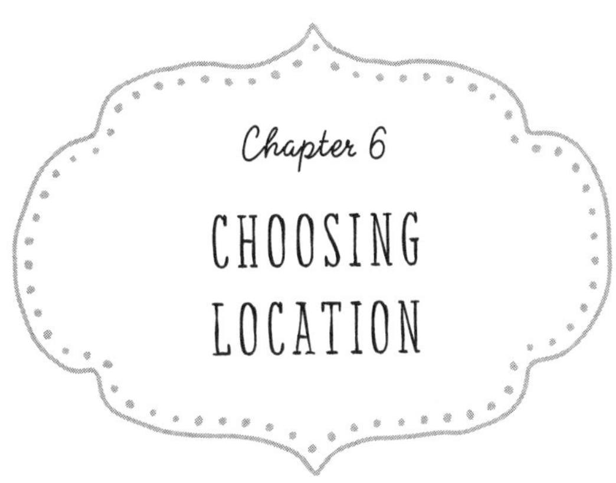

Chapter 6
CHOOSING LOCATION

Have you ever wondered where Adam and Eve made love? There's no master bedroom mentioned in Genesis.

As attached as we've gotten to our locked bedroom doors and cushy mattresses, there are plenty of other options for where a married couple can have sex. Let's explore the pros and cons of various locations.

> Let us go early to the vineyards
> to see if the vines have budded,
> if their blossoms have opened,
> and if the pomegranates are in bloom—
> there I will give you my love.
>
> Song of Songs 7:12

Where Not to Have Sex

We married people tend to be an unimaginative lot. After all, most couples have almost all of their sex in—*can you guess?*—a bed. And it makes sense, right? It's comfortable. There's a flexible mattress, cushy pillows, cool sheets, warm blankets, and plenty of space.

But you can introduce a little playfulness, creativity, or adventure into your sex life by varying where you have sex. Like the realtors say, consider location, location, location.

Besides atop the king mattress set, where else can a husband and wife be intimate? In the spirit of the medical ethics principle of *primum non nocere* ("First, do no harm"), let's focus first on places you *think* would be fun for sex, but in reality, not so much.

Elevator. The thought of being alone in an elevator with your hubby, stripping down, and doing it against the wall or on the floor as you go up or down sounds adventurous. In the movies, a lot of making out and sex goes on in elevators. There's even an Aerosmith song titled "Love in an Elevator."

However, many elevators these days have cameras. So unless you're trying to entertain the security guard with a free porn movie, why go there? Plus, you never know when the door might open for someone who's pressed the button on their floor. And if you push the red Stop button, you may be preventing someone from getting someplace they need to go. Finally, are you putting a plastic cover down, or messing up their carpet? I'm just sayin'.

Basically, an elevator is a moving closet. If you want that experience, put full-length mirrors along the walls of your closet, install a handrail, pipe in some easy-listening tunes, and pretend to push the Lobby button. Same thing, with no interruptions or photographic evidence.

Beach. Remember that famous scene in *From Here to Eternity* in which Burt Lancaster and Deborah Kerr roll around on the shore in each other's arms? The sun's rays beating down on you, the waves licking your bodies, the wind blowing through your hair. Could it get any sexier?

Now for the reality of sexual activity on the beach. Sand

gets everywhere. And I mean *everywhere*. If you think the worst place to pick grains of sand from is your ear canal, you are sadly mistaken. Throwing down a blanket won't stop that wonderful wind from blowing the sand your way. Plus, there are birds. You do not want a flock of seagulls watching you mate or dropping their souvenirs on your head.

Kitchen table. Another movie-inspired idea, I think. Thanks to Kevin Costner and Susan Sarandon in *Bull Durham*, a lot of women imagine their husbands clearing off a table and taking them, right then, right there. This could also be a desk, as many have imagined making love at one or the other's workplace.

News flash! Tables and desks are hard. It is not comfortable to have your hips, back, and derriere slammed against a surface that has as little give as a concrete sidewalk. Positioning yourself for intercourse is not always easy, and if your back and knees are over thirty years old, grab the pain reliever before you even begin.

Ground. Mosquitoes, chiggers, and ants, oh my! If you lay your naked bodies down on the dirt or grass, you can expect to make contact with nature. Sometimes nature is beautiful; sometimes it's harsh. You do not want to have an orgasm followed by poison ivy in the same place. Even if the sex is fabulous, is it worth scratching your nether regions for two weeks? Of course, this is preventable with a little planning.

Bring a quilt, a blanket, or at least a tarp. Put something between you and God's green earth. Yes, I know Song of Songs speaks of the married couple being in the vineyard and under the apple tree, but I imagine that smart chap having a bed linen at the ready.

In public. Several years ago, I found used condoms in our church parking lot. Very uncool. I had to get a latex glove and paper towels, grab the icky prophylactic, and trash it before a child could pick it up and ask, "What's this?" The offending party probably should not have been having sex to begin with (assuming that was fornication), but even if he was married, he could have chosen a more conducive location.

In reality, any place where children are present and could see you or your evidence is not an appropriate location for sex. There's a reason people advise, "Get a room."

Where to Try Having Sex

Varying the location where you make love can introduce a little spice into the experience. If you're looking for some place to have sex other than a bed, an elevator, the beach, the table, and—heaven forbid—a port-a-john (a terrible location one blog reader mentioned), where can you go? Here are some options.

Outside. Wait! Wasn't that on the no-no list? Yes. But the outdoors can be a beautiful setting for lovemaking, and the feel of a breeze on your skin can heighten arousal with your lover. The trick is to pick your outdoor location with care. Head to your backyard (assuming it's fenced), your porch or deck, or another private outdoor location. If you have a playground structure or tree house in your yard, try that. Bring a blanket or quilt to protect you from ant beds or poison ivy. Or set up a tent in your yard and camp out together. Let the moon provide the mood lighting and the birds, crickets, and cicadas provide the music.

Vehicle. Well, it depends on the vehicle. Those of you who drive a Smart Car should put this one in the last section's "not so much" category. And if you're in a classic Corvette, you'll find the stick shift gets in the way. In the United States, however, vehicles have gotten larger and larger, so if you drive a van, an SUV, or a truck, you likely have ample room to get it on in the backseat or truck bed.

Find an out-of-the-way location or even your garage, pack a romantic picnic, and turn on your car radio. Turn off the vehicle's engine and rev up your own. Pretty soon, it'll be humming and purring with delight. Steaming up the windows and shaking the car are added bonuses to this activity.

Chair in your house. Find a cushioned chair, not a hardback wooden one. A chair is a great place to vary your intimacy routine because there are sexual positions you can get into with the assistance of a chair that are not easily done on a bed. The wife can sit on her husband's lap, facing forward, or straddle him, facing the back of the chair. The couple can use the chair for leverage or kneeling. You could also use a bench seat for the same purpose.

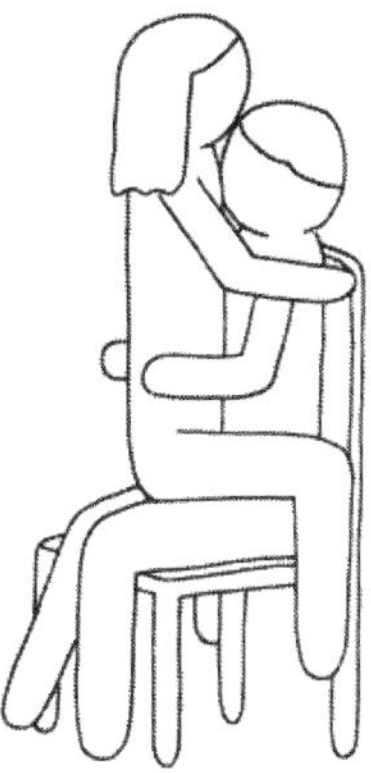

Use your imagination. Explore and figure out what works for you as a couple.

Water. By water, I mean any place where there is water: your shower, your bath, a hot tub, a river, the ocean, a pool. And by sex, I mean the whole kit and caboodle, not just intercourse. Adding a little H_2O to the lovemaking can be a scintillating experience. Just one caution: Showers, pools, and the like are fabulous places for foreplay, but not for penetration. It's difficult to get into a good position, surfaces are slippery, and water can wash away the necessary moisture for comfortable entry.

But go ahead and get naked and explore each other's bodies. Kiss and fondle. Lick and grope. There's something about the water against your skin that can enliven your senses and make you even more responsive to your spouse's touch. When you're ready for the finale, move the party to a more conducive location.

Cozy rug or blanket. I'm not talking about that scratchy oriental rug you bought at a garage sale and never cleaned. Or your childhood Holly Hobbie quilt. I'm talking about a soft fabric placed on the floor—maybe in front of a fireplace or covered with rose petals and lit with candles. Aaaaah, inviting.

Homemade fort. Just like you did as a kid, build a sheets-and-blankets fort and decorate it however you want. Make it your love den. Then climb inside and get going.

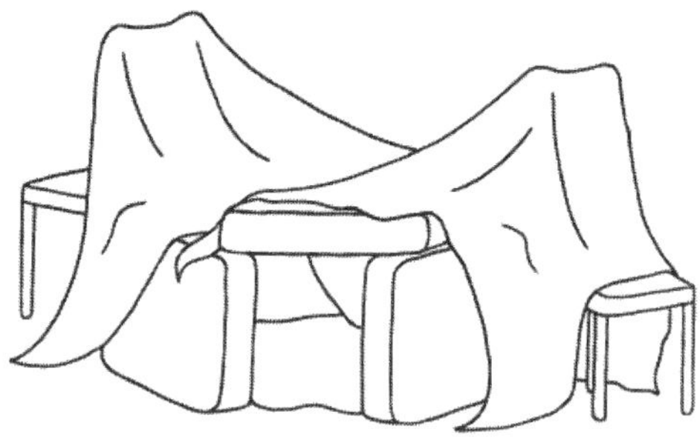

Boat. Actually, I don't know if a boat is a good place to have sex. It's just on my list of "I'd like to try it sometime." It seems like you'd need a big enough one to stay steady in the water, but a gentle rocking motion might be nice too.

Change up the location and see if that spices up your experience. If nothing else, you'll have that shared memory of "Remember when we ...?"

Chapter 7
INITIATING SEX

My husband is the master of bad sex-initiation lines. Thankfully, his wife has a sense of humor and finds his odd wordings amusing. Still, I keep a list of them and sometimes remind my hubby of what he said, which makes him laugh too. It becomes a shared funny memory.

Perhaps you and your husband are pros at initiation lines, or getting things started with no words needed. But lots of wives don't know whether they should initiate sex. Or they want some ideas for foreplay. So let's address both.

> Come away, my beloved,
> and be like a gazelle
> or like a young stag
> on the spice-laden mountains.
>
> Song of Songs 8:14

Should You Initiate Sex?

After seeing several surveys in which husbands reported wanting their wives to initiate sex, I wondered what exactly they meant. Do husbands want wives to be sexually aggressive or simply more receptive to their lead? Do they desire us to knock on that door or merely leave a key to come in when they want? Is it best to initiate sex or simply flirt with your husband so he'll get the idea?

I asked husbands, through Twitter and Facebook, to answer this question: *Do you prefer your wife to initiate sex or just to be enthusiastic when you initiate?*

Here's a sampling of the responses I received:

> YES and YES! Does it really have to be an either/or question? :-)

> I like it when she initiates, and I wouldn't want to say that I prefer her to do so. We should pursue each other sexually and not have only one initiating. I know that I jump for joy when she initiates, and it makes me feel great if I see and feel her enthusiasm when I initiate. It makes us both feel loved when the other is just as excited about making love, whoever started it.

> I agree with [the first answer]. I love it to be initiated. Lets me know she needs me as much as I need her. But if I do initiate and it's enthusiastically received, it's a real turn-on! Makes me we want to do more. Doesn't have to be that way every time, just like I do not have to be Mr. Romance Novel every time.

> I guess if I had to have a preference, I would say that I would prefer that she would be enthusiastic (not fake) rather than her initiating. Just knowing that she is really interested sends me over the top!

> Do I have to choose? Both are great. When I suggest it, there is always a chance of a negative response. But if she asks …

A happy & healthy blending of the two.

Either, anything, something!

What struck me about these answers is the reciprocity of sexual enthusiasm these husbands want. They want to know their wives desire them sexually.

In truth, we wives want to feel desired as well. Some women don't always understand it in sexual terms, but being pursued and focused on is a demonstration of love. When one of you in the marriage is always the one to initiate sex, it can feel like your spouse doesn't care—not just about desiring sex, but about desiring you.

Reciprocity matters. Can you imagine a friendship in which one of you always initiated contact or conversation? Would you feel valued if you were the only one who set up lunches or tennis dates or girls' weekends? What if you stopped pursuing that friendship and chose to wait on your friend? If that person never initiated, your relationship would likely fade into oblivion.

You certainly don't want that to happen to your marital intimacy.

It needn't be a 50/50 proposition. One of you (in friendship or in marriage) may be the natural starter, the go-getter in personality or desire. The other may be happy to engage but more comfortable in a receptive role. That's okay. But it's worth shaking that up occasionally. Sometimes the non-starter should initiate and let his/her spouse know the desire is mutual.

Freshen Up Your Foreplay

A few years ago, my husband and I took swing dance classes. It took a while to get the basic steps down, leaving little opportunity to add much else to our repertoire. Consequently, while we can swing dance a bit, it's mostly a 1-2-3-4 count in our heads and not a lot of flare. We enjoy getting out on the dance floor, but it would be fun to freshen up our footwork.

Do you feel that way about sexual foreplay in your marriage? Like you've got your moves down, but you revisit the same 1-2-3-4 steps again and again? How can you freshen up your foreplay?

Get Romantic. Add some romance to your repertoire. What sexual moves convey *l'amour* to you? Consider the following ideas:

Turn on some music and dance a slow dance that arouses your senses and melds your bodies.

Give each other body massages or even a sensual massage of your private areas. Find a massage lotion or oil you like, perhaps one with aromatherapy elements.

Take a bubble bath together. Spend time in each other's arms, soaking in the tub or soaping each other up.

Light candles and set the mood for a beautiful night of lovemaking.

Wear something romantic, like a peignoir set (that's the silky nightgown with matching robe), and dab on a little perfume.

Get Creative. In addition to trying new positions and locations, maybe you could try one of these activities.

Grab some props. Gather a few items that let you to experiment with texture or temperature—like a feather, heat packs, sensory massage balls, a silk scarf, an ice cube or chilled hard-boiled egg. Take turns exploring the sensations as you touch each other's bodies with the items.

Introduce food into your sexual play. Feed each other strawberries. Tease with whipped cream. Lick off edible body paint.

Go blindfolded. Grab bandannas and blindfold each other,

then feel your way through the foreplay. Let your hands do the talking.

Get Playful. Foreplay can be a playful, even humorous, experience. Welcome mutual laughter into your marriage bed. Here are a few ideas to try:

Use a board game as part of your foreplay. Several board games for couples focus on sex. One of my favorites is Bliss. (Note: Some activities in these games might make you uncomfortable. So agree up front that either of you can skip one and try another card/roll/etc.) But you can play any game, from Battleship (sinking ships earns sexual goodies) to Twister (right on red, bodies entangled) to the tried-and-true Strip Poker.

Introduce word play into your flirtation and advances. Can you come up with puns or phrases that make you both smile and anticipate lovemaking?

Tickle each other. Not the way your big brother did when you were little and you cried "uncle" so he'd stop. But find those places on each other's bodies that make you smile and giggle a bit, and then play with them.

Grab a Nerf gun. Actually, this is a good motto for all of life. If all else fails, grab a Nerf gun and see how that can improve your mood. Even load that baby up with water and squirt away at each other.

Get spiritual. Have you ever brought God into the bedroom in a big way? How about reminding yourselves how spiritual the sexual experience is? Not sure how to do that? Try these suggestions:

Pull out a Bible and open it to Song of Songs (also called Song of Solomon). Read through the book together. It can be quite titillating.

Pray over each other's bodies. Start with the head, then extremities, torso, and finally the pleasure spots. Explore each place sensually, praying over each God-given body part, and then pleasure that spot thoroughly before moving on.

Use these suggestions, or think outside the box and come up with your own ideas to freshen your foreplay.

Chapter 8
ORAL SEX

You want me to put my mouth where?!"

That's the gut response of many wives when they first contemplate giving oral sex. It seems natural to match up genitalia, but when it comes to your mouth, that's a whole different story. Sure, you love his manhood and all, but you wonder: Is that allowed? Is it healthy? Is it sanitary? Is it biblical? Is it worth it?

My beloved has gone down to his garden,
to the beds of spices,
to browse in the gardens and to gather lilies.

Song of Songs 6:2

Is Oral Sex Okay with God?

Of course, we want any sexual activity we do in our marriage bed to be acceptable to our Creator. So we should begin first with whether oral sex is approved by God.

According to most modern biblical scholars, the Song of Songs is about the sexual love between a married couple. In this Old Testament book, preserved as part of the Holy Scriptures, specific sexual acts are described. There appear to be at least two references to oral sex—the first woman to man, the second man to woman.

"Like an apple tree among the trees of the forest, so is my beloved among the young men. In his shade I took great delight and sat down, and his fruit was sweet to my taste" (Song of Songs 2:3 NASB). "Fruit" is a euphemism, of course.

"Awake, O north wind, and come, wind of the south; make my garden breathe out fragrance, let its spices be wafted abroad. May my beloved come into his garden and eat its choice fruits!" (Song of Songs 4:16 NASB).

Thus, there is no prohibition against oral sex. Rather, it appears to have been part of the sexual relationship between this biblical husband and wife.

Moreover, there is nothing inherently harmful about oral sex. There isn't much research into the composition or possible health benefits, but a wife's natural lubricant appears to be okay for her husband to ingest. The same is true for the wife ingesting her husband's secretions. One study even suggested semen has antidepressant qualities.[13] (Go figure.)

Contact of lips and tongue to genitals is not much different from that of hands or fingers. No stretching or painful penetration are involved.*

The one caveat is that sexually transmitted diseases and infections can be passed by oral-genital contact, so if that is an issue in your marriage, be aware.

With possible biblical precedent and no harmful side effects, what are the objections to oral sex? Some believe it is unnatural to engage in a sexual activity that doesn't involve

* The same cannot be said of anal sex. The rectum contains harmful bacteria, is not designed for penetration, and usually involves pain for the woman.

penetration. However, sexual encounters involve foreplay, which isn't penetration.

Some people think oral sex is wrong because it is portrayed in pornography. Well, so is intercourse. While I strongly warn against viewing pornography and attempting to copy what is seen there, plenty of people who've never watched a porn film engage in fellatio and cunnilingus. They didn't get the idea from porn.

It's fine for a couple to kiss each other's bodies, right? So where must the lips stop kissing? Before reaching genitalia? Inner thigh okay but vulva not? Without biblical, health, or practical reasons, I don't see why that area is forbidden.

There is no rule that you must have oral sex as part of an intimate relationship. Plenty of sexually satisfied couples don't. You must decide for yourself and live according to your conscience before God. Just don't allow preconceived notions to decide for you. Search it out for yourself. Decide based on the merits whether oral sex will be on your marital intimacy menu.

For Him (Fellatio)

Here's a glimpse into my internal conversation while I prepared my first blog post on oral sex:

Me: *I should do a post on giving blow jobs.*
I: *What are you going to say about them?*
Me: *You know, a how-to.*
I: *You're going to describe how to give a blow job? Are you crazy!*
Me: *Some wives might want a little coaching.*
I: *Are you actually going to call it a "blow job"?*

Me: *That's what everyone calls it.*
I: *How about "fellatio"?*
Me: *If I call it fellatio, no one will know what I'm talking about.*
I: *How about "the thing that must not be named"?*
Me: *Isn't that Voldemort from Harry Potter?*
I: *Your brain is too distracted.*
Me: *Not when I'm giving a blow job. I'm really focused then. You know, "his fruit is sweet to my taste," from Song of Songs?*
I: *So that you don't choke?*
Me: *Well, yeah. And because it's kinda hot.*
I: *So you're actually going to talk about this in public?*
Me: *Um, maybe.*
I: *Well, if you do, don't take me down with you.*
Me: *"Take me down." That's funny.*
I: *(rolls eyes)*

Sources that describe how to give a "blow job" usually do not have a Christian perspective and may use photography or graphic images. Perhaps some people have learned how to do it from watching a porn film. As I've said, I have never seen a porn film. (I put it in the ranks of heroin. I don't need to try it to know I don't need to try it.) But, through research and experience, I have gained wisdom about this activity over the years.

Some husbands would like their wives to "go down" on them, and some wives would be willing to give it a shot or want to try it again. But they may not think they know what to do or how to do it. So ready or not, here I go with a short how-to lesson on giving a blow job.

Do you actually blow? No. Please do not treat your husband's opening like the end of a balloon and attempt to inflate it with your breath. A blow job is merely the slang term for a woman inserting a man's penis into her mouth. What happens after that determines whether it is a good blow job or a lame one.

How much of his penis do I put in my mouth? You can put your mouth only around the head of the penis, move your mouth over the shaft, or deep-throat your husband's entire penis (explained below). This isn't about swallowing your husband. It's about providing oral stimulation to his sensitive genital area. While providing oral stimulation, you will need to breathe mostly through your nose.

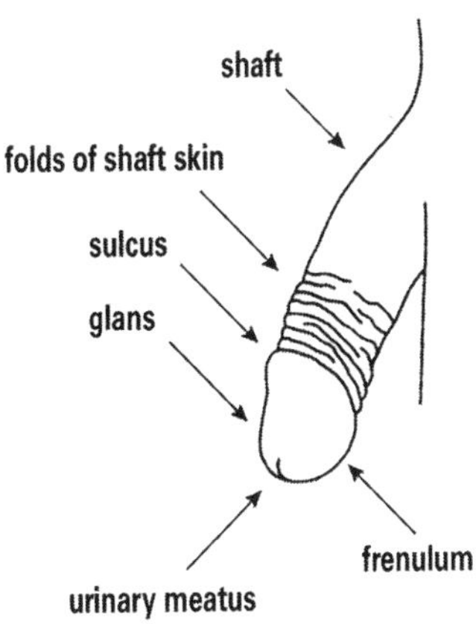

What do I do with my mouth? Kiss, lick, and suck with your lips and tongue. Use the tongue to give small licks around the ridge, head, and tip, or longer licks up and down the shaft of the penis. With the penis inside your mouth, you can pump your tongue a little to increase pressure. Sucking also increases the pressure, especially as you move your mouth up and down his penis. You can add your hand to the mix; that is, simultaneously use your hand(s) to provide slight pressure and a different feel as your mouth works.

For the first time out, imagine the head of the penis as an ice cream cone and the shaft as a Fudgsicle. That might help a little.

Where does it feel best for him? The greatest concentration of nerve endings is in the head of a man's penis. While stimulating the shaft also feels good, the ridge between the shaft and head, the head itself, and the tip are all more sensitive. Licking, sucking, and oral pressure in that area will feel particularly good. That said, you can't just hang out there doing the same thing over and over. The best sex involves variation, and that goes for oral sex as well.

What is "deep-throating"? That expression means to put the penis so far into your mouth that the head makes contact with your throat. The throat is a tighter space than your mouth and can provide more pressure and friction.

Here's some advice if you want to give it a try. Open your throat and widen your mouth to an aperture larger than your husband's penis so that you can continue to breathe around it. You don't need to stay in that position for long. Throating the tip and then moving back out may feel better to your husband anyway.

Should I spit or swallow? Some women don't want semen in their mouths, period—either because they do not want to waste the sperm (a principle in Catholicism) or because they are repulsed by the thought of this liquid in their mouths. If you are one of them, you'll need to make sure you pull your mouth away well in advance. If your husband reaches the "point of no return," he will begin ejaculation whether your mouth is there or not.

If you are willing to allow your husband's ejaculate into your mouth but don't want to swallow, be polite about spitting it out. You might be offended if your husband gave you oral sex but made a big deal about disliking your natural lubrication. Have a cup handy somewhere nearby, hold the liquid in your mouth, and then spit it into the cup. Or use a hand towel. You can always go to the bathroom to brush your teeth and/or use mouthwash to clear out the taste.

However, you might simply want to swallow. Ingesting semen is not in any way harmful to your body. The consistency of semen is like a beaten egg. The taste ranges from sweet to salty. It contains vitamins, sodium, and fructose. If you're worried about your waistline, don't be. Semen ranges between five to twenty-five calories[14]—hardly a diet killer.

What if I give my husband a blow job, and I don't like it? Ask yourself what you didn't enjoy about the experience. Did you dislike certain sensations? Did your jaw hurt? Is the problem something that could be adjusted the next time around?

If you genuinely do not want to engage in this activity in the future, tell your husband. Try not to say something like "That was so yuck!" He may take it personally that you don't want to make oral contact with his manhood. Simply explain that you felt very uncomfortable, and you prefer other activities as part of your sex life. You might even suggest one. Perhaps you don't want to perform fellatio, but you're willing to do a striptease for him or introduce an appropriate sex toy or give him a hand job.

How can my husband help to make this a positive experience? The first caveat is that you should be allowed to remain in control of your mouth. If you need to pull away and take a break, he should understand that. In a moment of extreme pleasure, a man might want to hold his wife's head and pull her mouth onto him. This often isn't a good idea; men are stronger than they sometimes realize, and this action can make it difficult for the woman to control the motions in such a way that she remains comfortable throughout.

Your husband should also communicate about what feels good to him. He can talk you through it or make happy noises when you've hit a really great spot. You can even talk ahead of time so he can show you on his penis where his most pleasurable places are. Afterward you can discuss how it felt so you know what worked best and what he might like next time.

Finally, he can affirm you. We women like to be appreciated when we go out of our way to do something. Well, here's an opportunity for a husband to say nice things about his wife for her willingness to focus the sexual experience on his pleasure.

Some wives actually get a lot of pleasure from giving blow jobs. Remember Song of Songs 2:3?

> Like an apple tree among the trees of the forest is my
> lover among the young men.
> I delight to sit in his shade,
> and his fruit is sweet to my taste.

For Her (Cunnilingus)

Want another peek into my brain? (Be afraid. Be very afraid.)

Me: *What should I call this post?*

I: *How about "Lie Back and Think of England"?*

Me: *No. That's what that crazy British lady said to make women think sex isn't enjoyable. How about "Lie Back and Think of Tinglin'"? That's more like it!*

I: *Seriously?*

Me: *Sorta seriously. Or I could just call it "Goin' Down." Bow chicka wow-wow.*

I: *You are going down ... into the gutter, girlfriend. What's wrong with you?*

Me: *Quite a few things. For one, I can't cook all that well. Plus, my nose is kind of big. And my—*

I: *No, no. I mean, why do you always joke about sex?*

Me: *Um … 'cause it's funny?*

I: *You think sex is funny?*

Me: *Don't you? Hey, I'm about to tell a group of Christian wives why spreading their legs and letting their hubbies' mouths touch their private parts can be kinda nice. I'm even going to tell them that it's in the Bible! I sure didn't know that when I was a teen. If this subject had been mentioned in my "becoming a woman" Bible class, I would have fallen out of my chair from embarrassment or laughter or both.*

I: *You're digressing. How about "Oral Sex: Better to Give and Receive"?*

Me: *I like it! Let's go with that.*

Believe it or not, a lot of hubbies would like to get their wives tinglin' down there. Several husbands have reported on my blog that they are physically aroused and emotionally moved by the openness of their wives when *she* is on the receiving end of oral sex.

Yet plenty of wives are nervous, resistant, or downright opposed to cunnilingus (the scientific term for a woman receiving oral sex). For whatever reason, the idea of their husband's mouth on their privates does not sound appealing. As with fellatio, I'm going to give some basic information. Perhaps after learning more about it, you may open up to the experience—figuratively and literally.

What's so pleasurable about oral sex for a woman? First of all, the focus is on the wife. While sex should be mutually satisfying, there are benefits to focusing on one spouse or the other from time to time. A husband can get a big kick out of getting his wife's engine purring.

Second, it is a different and delicate sensation. Back to my ice cream cone example. Have you ever held an ice cream cone and eaten it this way and that way? You can slurp with your tongue all the way across. Give little licks along the edge or at the whipped top. Suck the cream with your mouth. Twirl your tongue around. Brush your lips against the coolness. Come at the ice cream straight on, sideways, or from any other angle. Now imagine you are the ice cream. Can you see why that might feel good?

Third, many husbands like that perspective. A man's eyes are close to his mouth, so he can see what he's doing, gauge your body's response, and revel in your pleasure. Let me cite some husbands' comments from my blog about the appeal of giving cunnilingus:

> She is totally open to me, and I am giving her incredible pleasure.
>
> I've always loved giving my wife oral sex. It is probably my favorite thing to do.
>
> She is then totally open, giving herself totally over to me.
>
> I am a husband who loves going down on my wife. I really enjoy experiencing her orgasm from that perspective. It is truly amazing.

Fourth, it is one of the easier ways for a woman to orgasm, which I'll cover in a bit.

What do you need to do to enjoy receiving oral sex? Just "lie back and think of tinglin'"? Sort of. Because you need to relax. A wife who has never engaged in oral sex, or who has been unable to enjoy receiving it, may tense when her husband starts to "go down" on her. We have all kinds of thoughts: *Do I want his mouth on my girly parts? Is this clean? What do I smell like down there? What do I look like down there? Eyes up here, buddy; don't look at my thunder thighs! Does this make me a slut? What does God think of this? What do I think of this?*

While the wife is having thoughts like these, here's what the husband is thinking: *Sex. Wife. Vulva. Sweet. Love.*

If only we could live in a guy's brain for a minute or two, we could relax too.

Shut off the distractions, train yourself to open up to the sensations your body is feeling, and go with the flow. Let your husband turn you on. When you open your body up to him and to sexual pleasure, you are beautiful and sexy to him.

How can you help it go well? Learn your body. Know your anatomy and where stimulation is likely to feel good. The most pleasurable part of a woman's anatomy is the clitoris, a knobby bit of flesh at the top of the genitalia. Doctors and researchers report that this area must be stimulated directly or indirectly for a woman to orgasm. But the labia minora are also quite sensitive to touch.

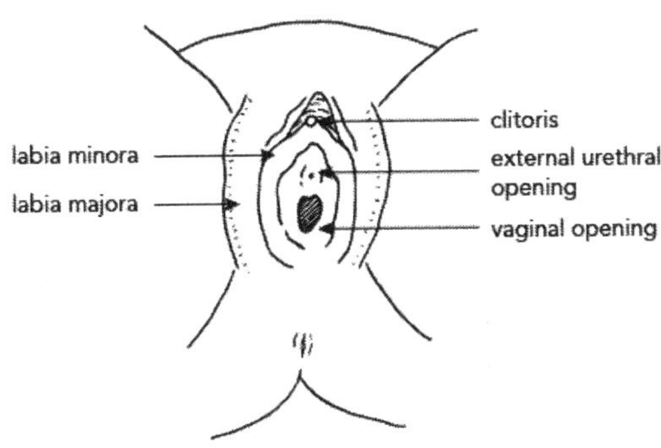

As you think about what feels good, give your husband directions. Not as in "A little to the left, buddy. No, not there! Ouch. Can't you do anything right? I said the left. Your other left!" Instead, gently let your husband know what feels good. You can moan, groan, whisper, ooh, aah, talk, gyrate, purr, or even roar—whatever suits your fancy. You can adjust his head so his lips and tongue contact you in a delightful place. You can use your hand to open up your vaginal lips and give him more direct access. Some wives (and husbands) claim that shaving or waxing that area increases sensation and arousal; other wives are not comfortable with that. Also, you might want to take a bath or shower right beforehand to make sure everything is clean down there and smells nice.

You may wish to talk to your husband about this ahead of time. Let him know he needs to go slow. It does not feel good to most wives to have hubby go down and start brashly licking or sucking the clitoris. We need time to build up. He can begin by kissing your lips, your body, your thighs, and then move to the genital area. The lips and tongue should be used to tease for a while before pressure is increased. After a while of slow stimulation, you may want him to increase the speed and/or pressure of his mouth's action against your skin.

Will you climax? Maybe. Because the husband can directly stimulate the clitoris, the mouth provides lubrication with saliva, and the tongue's pressure can vary in intensity, many wives report experiencing climax during oral sex. Whether or not you climax, oral sex is likely to feel good.

Some couples use oral sex as foreplay. In fact, when a wife approaches climax, she may feel a strong desire for penetration. You can allow climax to occur during oral stimulation from your husband or move to intercourse and perhaps experience an orgasm after entry.

For women, there are no guarantees for having an orgasm during sexual encounters. In fact, that's not the purpose of marital intimacy. It is about closeness and pleasure. Yet the paradox is that if you focus on your relationship and pleasurable sensations, you are more likely to have an orgasm.

Focus on pleasure, enjoy the sensations, and delight that your lover wants to please you in that way. You might find cunnilingus is a great addition to your sexual intimacy.

What if you just don't wanna? If the thought of receiving oral sex sickens you, or violates your conscience, or you simply don't enjoy the experience, don't do it. Godly sexuality is never about forcing or demanding sexual acts from your spouse. If you don't want to have oral sex, find other activities that are mutually pleasurable.

The beauty of intimacy in marriage is that, while there are some restrictions, there is a substantial amount of freedom. You can spend the next fifty years getting to know each other's bodies and engaging in physical intimacy that makes your body tingle, your heart pump, and your connection deepen.

Still Nervous about Giving Him Oral?

If you're still nervous about giving your husband a blow job, I get it. Let's talk girlfriend-to-girlfriend and break down some wives' concerns.

Is it hygienic? This is a big concern for many, especially since the penis is also used for urinating. It can seem unsanitary to put your mouth where urine has been. However, when a man ejaculates, a muscle contracts in the neck of the bladder, preventing urine flow into the penis—meaning a man cannot shoot semen and urine at the same time.

Not to be gross here, but even if a minuscule amount of urine did enter your mouth by some off chance, it's not unhealthy for you. Urine is mostly waste-filtered water, and while you don't want to be ingesting much, a teeny bit isn't harmful.

Still, you may feel it's not very sanitary. Perhaps you're concerned that his groin area can sweat during the day. If cleanliness is your concern, ask hubby to take a thorough shower before you begin, or at least wash his genitals. You can even suggest a bath together, and do the washing yourself so you know that area is spic-and-span.

Oh, and if hair bothers you, ask him to do a bit of "manscaping." Believe it or not, plenty of husbands do it. Your husband might be willing to trim a bit, just like he'd trim a mustache or beard. It doesn't hurt to ask. Still, getting his pubic hair in your mouth is the same as getting any of his other hair in your mouth.

Is it all or nothing? When you hear about oral sex for him, you likely picture his penis all the way in your mouth. But that term, "oral sex" only means using your mouth to stimulate his genitalia. That's it. You have many other options you can explore.

It doesn't have to look like a classic "blow job" for your husband to enjoy your mouth on his manhood. God made that skin on your husband so sensitive. He may be thrilled for your lips to simply kiss and lick the soft head of his penis. Your tongue licking the length of his shaft may send him right over the edge. He might adore you adding mouth contact while you're giving him a hand job, or while he's taking care of that part, stacking one pleasure on top of another.

You can put his penis into your mouth, or you can find other ways to enjoy oral sex. Just start with light kisses and see how things progress.

Is it worth trying? Your husband probably thinks so. And we want to consider our mates when it comes to the marriage bed.

The real question is, do *you* think it's worth trying? If you don't have moral or hygienic objections, what's holding you back? It could be nervousness about what it will feel like, concern you won't do it right, worry that you'll gag, or fear of him expecting you to swallow. Communicate your concerns to your husband and tell him that you're willing to try but you need to go slow and stay in control of how this goes.

Let him express to you what feels good, and be willing to adjust according to what he likes and what feels okay to you. You may discover that the skin really isn't that different from other parts of his body (except how soft it is) or that you're actually excited by how effectively your mouth arouses your husband.

If you enjoy it, you can do it more. If you feel awkward or uncomfortable, you can take a break, then try again. Or you can suggest turning to another sexual activity to finish, like a hand job or intercourse.

Trying a new sexual activity once doesn't mean you have to do it again and again. But you might find out that, with an open mind and some practice, you like giving him oral sex—that it arouses you as well. So yeah, it could be worth trying.

Chapter 9
THE HANDS-ON EXPERIENCE

Have you ever considered how handy your opposable thumbs are? Being able to hold, grasp, squeeze, and stroke with our hands is a wonderful aspect of our human bodies. Husbands and wives can even use their hands to bring great pleasure to each other.

His arms are rods of gold
set with topaz.
His body is like polished ivory
decorated with lapis lazuli.

Song of Songs 5:14

How Do You Like to Be Touched?

You might know how it feels to be lying in bed at night, reading a book, thumbing through a magazine, or even starting to doze off, and suddenly *Boom!* Your husband's hand clamps down on your breast or butt cheek like a claw from one of those toy grabber machines. *Hey, buddy! You did not insert a token, and I am not a stuffed animal!*

This is one of the biggest complaints I've heard from wives about sex—that their husbands don't know how to touch them.

Guess what? That means you have to teach him. Yes, almost every husband is teachable. And he will appreciate a lesson that involves this hands-on learning far better than any high school course he ever had.

Start the introduction outside the bedroom. When one of my children took Spanish, the teacher's lesson plan on the first day included this objective: "Discuss why it's important to learn Spanish." In the same manner, explain to your husband that it's important he learn how to touch you in a way that makes you feel cherished and that awakens your desire. Find someplace away from the bedroom to start the conversation in a neutral way, without immediate pressure to perform.

Tell him what benefits he will reap from this plan: that you expect to be more open to his advances if you first feel he loves *all* of you, not just the "good parts." Talk about how touching each other in the way you each want to be touched will increase your feelings of intimacy. Then announce that you want to practice, and even that you will need to practice a lot.

Show him in the bedroom. It's lab time, and you will be graded on a curve—a woman's curve, that is. Take time to talk about how and where you like to be touched. Show your husband by moving his hand or demonstrating with your own hand if you wish. Ask hubby if he's willing to keep touching you in the way you instruct until you get to the point of saying, "Touch the goodies!"

He might be surprised to find you're a willing participant in sexual intimacy if you have received the full-body touches you desire and require to heat up sufficiently. Women can require fifteen to twenty minutes of foreplay to be ready for penetration.

Fellow marriage blogger and author Sheila Wray Gregoire has made the wonderful point that wives often think they are not interested in sex because they aren't … at first.[15] Typically, females get interested in sex after they spend some time being attended to and aroused.

It's like men are sexual morning people—you know, those folks who wake up with a bolt at the first sign of sunlight through the window and they're ready for the day. Women are more like groggy morning people when it comes to sex—taking their time to rouse slowly and stretch and yawn and get the blood flowing where it needs to go to have energy for the day. But the blood can get flowing with the right touch.

Touch him the way he wants. As uncomfortable as it can feel the first time, try grabbing your husband's crotch when he isn't expecting it. Not too hard, of course; you don't want to damage the goods. The next time you embrace, move your hands down and squeeze his behind. When you go to bed, roll over and start fondling his testicles. Do you think you might get a positive response?

An ongoing message I hear from hubbies is that they want their wives to desire them sexually. While we ladies want to be desired non-sexually a lot of times, your man may very well be longing for you to show interest in his sexuality—in those external parts that make him a sexual being. Of course, plenty of husbands are still interested in holding hands, hugging, kissing, and making out, but now and then you might focus on that mid-section and see what reaction you draw.

Also, men typically want greater pressure applied in touch. You can be pretty firm with touching your husband's body and, specifically, his penis (although be very gentle with those tender testicles). Ask your hubby what amount of pressure feels good.

These are gender generalities, but you need to talk with your husband to see what he likes. Together, you can figure out how to best touch each other to get things going and feel cherished in the marriage bed.

How to Give a Hand Job

For many years, I could confidently say I was a good lover … except when it came to hand jobs. I was downright flummoxed.

I can't be the only wife who didn't know how to give her husband a great hand job. But it's good to have this in your marital intimacy repertoire for those times when intercourse is off limits due to a menstrual period or health restrictions or when you merely want some nice foreplay.

How do you give your husband a great hand job? I have learned a thing or two I'd like to share with you.

Lubricant. Rubbing your hand over his penis repeatedly may not feel good without moisture. Grab some lubricant. You can use one that is oil based (like coconut oil), water based (like Astroglide or KY), or silicone based (like Wet Platinum or Sliquid Silver). Find one you both like and start the hand job by applying a reasonable amount to your husband's penis and to your hands. Keep it nearby in case you need more.

Teasing. Take it slow at first. You can take your time undressing your husband and teasing him with your hands outside his clothes or underwear beforehand. Once he's bare, there are several ways to drive him a little crazy with gentle touching. You can touch or lick the head of his penis, lightly massage his testicles, or use your fingers to softly stroke his penis.

Body position. A hand job can be given from several positions. Your husband can sit in a chair while you kneel; he can lie down while you straddle-sit on his thighs; you can sit next to each other and you can reach over to touch him; you can lie in opposite directions with your head in line with his hips. If you have difficulty in one position, try another. Your respective heights and body comfort will make some positions more pleasant and conducive to arousal than others.

The view. Consider the view he's getting while you're in each body position. Your husband may respond even more to your touching if he's getting a pleasing visual. Most men are aroused by seeing their wives' bodies, in part or in full. While you're giving him the hand job, he may enjoy looking at your breasts, your derriere, or other pretty parts. Or perhaps he simply wants to gaze into your eyes. As the husband says in Song of Songs 1:15, "How beautiful you are, my darling! Oh, how beautiful! Your eyes are doves."

Hand positions. There are several different ways to position your hands. You can stroke up and down, up only with two hands alternating, twist your hand or hands back and forth around the shaft. You can use your whole hand, your palms only, or your fingers. Or pinch your finger and thumb together to form a ring (think of the okay sign).

Like sexual positions, some people have named various hand job moves, such as "the corkscrew" or "the pancake." But all of them are variations of the grip and stroke you use and the area you touch. There isn't one right hand position for giving a good hand job. As they say, different strokes for different folks. (Now I've ruined that saying for you, haven't I?)

Sensitivity. You may be tempted to concentrate on the shaft of the penis, since constantly stroking it can evoke ejaculation. However, the most sensitive part is the head, or glans, of the penis. Be sure to playfully and lovingly touch your husband's head, paying special attention to the frenulum—which appears like a stretch of taut skin running from the inner head of the penis to the shaft. The corona, or rim of the penis head, is also sensitive to touch.

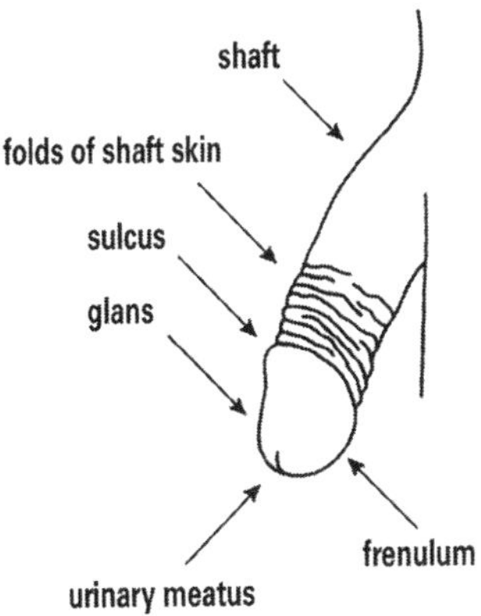

Rhythm. When your husband thrusts inside you, there's a rhythm to it, right? Well, you'll want to maintain a rhythm to your touching. It doesn't have to be consistent throughout; in fact, vary a little. You can start slow, increase the pace, slow again, increase, and so forth. Or just move from slower to faster. But don't stop and start; keep it going.

Climax. Decide together how you want to handle ejaculation. Do you want him to climax with the hand job? Do you want him to penetrate you when he's close? Do you want to maybe add your mouth to the equation? If you want to finish him with the hand job, you'll likely need to increase the pace and pressure as he comes close. You may also want to surround his penis with your whole hand (or two hands) to provide sensation all around for him. Pay attention to his cues. Is he tensing up? Asking for more? Making noises that indicate growing pleasure? Adjust your position and tension accordingly.

One more thing about climax. While it's incredibly enjoyable to most husbands to have their wives fondle and stroke the penis, it's a little more difficult for some husbands to reach orgasm that way. Your husband may prefer to move to penetration or even to take over some of the rhythm with his own hand. This is not a reflection on how good your hand feels to him. Talk about your expectations in advance and decide what's important to you both.

Communication. The best advice for giving your husband a fabulous hand job should come from your husband. He knows what feels good to his body. Encourage him to tell you what he likes or guide your hand(s). Let him know that you want to learn. I bet that statement alone—"Honey, will you show me how to give you a fabulous hand job?"—would cause plenty of husbands to come to attention.

Asking your husband how you can please him falls under one of the foundational principles to a truly intimate and enjoyable physical relationship in your marriage. The Bible's commands are relevant to every area of our lives, including the marital bedroom. So even though Philippians 2:3–4 isn't a scripture that addresses sexuality, consider the attitude we should take toward others: "Do nothing out of selfish ambition or vain conceit. Rather, in humility value others above yourselves, not looking to your own interests but each of you to the interests of the others."

It's a gift to your husband to let go of your selfishness, value his pleasure above your own, and look to his interests. The paradox is, a wife's own pleasure often multiplies when she asks how she can serve her mate and then pleasures him accordingly. And the same is true for husbands.

Manual Play for Her

Most wives enjoy their husbands touching them with deep embraces and gentle caresses, but what about something more titillating? How can a husband use his hands to stir up his wife's desire and give her oodles of pleasure?

Manual play refers to your hubby using his hands on your genitalia to arouse and satisfy you sexually. There's quite a bit he can do down there with his talented, God-given hands. Let's talk about a few approaches. If something here intrigues you, invite your husband to give it a try.

Rub-a-dub-dub. Hubby can use his fingers or whole hand to rub your privates. This might feel best away from the most sensitive areas, like the clitoris, instead focusing on either side of your vulva or the "mound," or mons pubis, above the genitals. The right pressure is important, and he should probably approach it like a massage stroke.

Tease and please. His fingers can be used with soft strokes to tease and please all of the areas of your pleasure places. One tip most men need is to go slow. Sometimes a husband can get antsy wanting to rev things up quickly and get you to that powerful peak. However, women usually respond better by warming up slowly and enjoying all the lovely sensations along the way. Let him know this is a tease-fest, and you want him to stay with it until you beg for more.

Round and round he goes. Circles are very easy to explain to hubby and can feel very good to wifey. Where can he circle his hand or fingers? How about around your vulva? The perimeter of your vaginal opening? Your clitoris? All of those places would likely respond to circular motion with his hands.

Slip-n-slide. Let him slip his finger into your vagina—that's called "digital penetration." Usually, the finger that works best is the middle one, because of its flexibility and the rest of the hand stabilizing it. Using that finger also allows him to have other fingers free to stroke or rub the area outside as well. If you'd like, he can add another finger or two, increasing the friction and sense of fullness. He can caress your vagina, thrust in and out to mimic intercourse, or hook his finger toward the front and try to locate your G-spot. If he can find it (no guarantee, but worth a shot), your pleasure will likely build even more with direct contact to that sensitive site.

What's the goal of manual play? Primarily, it's foreplay. It should be a huge turn-on to you and to him for you to be touched. In this way, your husband can explore your tender places and get to know your body more fully. Meanwhile, you can experience the pleasurable sensations of being lovingly touched in your most private area.

Manual play is also a fabulous way to get your lubrication going. In order to have intercourse, you need to be "wet." If he can stimulate you first with his hands, then he can reach in a bit, draw out your natural lubrication, and spread it over your vulva. If you're not producing much on your own, you can grab some personal lubricant and use it during manual play, or introduce it before intercourse. Your manual play might actually feel better with some added wetness to get things moving.

Manual play is a great method of reaching climax. Many wives respond well to their husband's hands stimulating them down below. Quite frankly, a hand can be more precise and adaptive than a penis. Thus, if you need a certain level of pressure or for him to *hit that right spot*, having him "finger" you might be the best way to nudge you up that climax cliff and send you over the edge.

This position can also be very enjoyable for a husband, because he gets to watch the entire thing. Most hubbies love seeing their wives experience that wave of excitement, and knowing he did it all with his hand is a pretty awesome *attaboy* he can give himself.

A few last-minute tips for manual play, to make sure things go smoothly.

Give him access. For years, I didn't think our girly parts were all that pretty, so I wasn't super-willing to show them off to my hubby. He doesn't see it that way. Regardless of how we feel about ourselves down there, we need to embrace our husbands' fascination with our goodies. Hubby likely thinks it's an amusement park down there, and he's itching to pay his ticket and see the sights. So let him. Share your feminine beauty by breathing easily, opening up, and letting him see and touch this special part of your God-woven body.

Use lubricant. Your own natural juices or purchased personal lubricant or coconut oil will help your husband's hands glide across your private places, and the contact will feel much better to you. After a bit of stimulation, you can invite your husband to swirl his finger into your opening and draw out the wetness there to share with the rest of your area.

Go slow. Make sure he knows this isn't a race. You want to enjoy his hands and fingers fondling you, so ask him to give you time to bask in his talents and your sensations. Your arousal will be heightened if he can start slow and build the speed, pressure, and intensity as your body responds to his touch.

Remember the clitoris. The clitoris is a particularly sensitive area of your privates. It's a knobby bit of flesh at the top of your vagina that swells when highly aroused. Climaxes occur when the clitoris is directly or indirectly stimulated, and manual play can take real advantage of that. Your husband can see directly when he's hitting that spot and lean into that pleasure for you. Show him exactly where you want to be touched, pointing out the location of your clitoris and the type of strokes that feel best.

Manual play can be an exciting part of your lovemaking. Add it to your foreplay, use it to explore and experience orgasm, and let your husband be hands-on with you. Pay attention to the beautiful sensations that emerge, and thank God for the fabulous skill of hands.

Chapter 10
SEXUAL FANTASIES

One definition *Random House Dictionary* gives for *fantasy* is "the forming of mental images, especially wondrous or strange fancies; imaginative conceptualizing." What "wondrous or strange fancies" come to your mind or your husband's when it comes to your sexual intimacy? What "imaginative conceptualizing" might there be for sexual encounters between you two? God gave us incredible imaginations, but He also set before us some responsibilities regarding our thought life and our behaviors. So what should you do with sexual fantasies?

> Finally, brothers and sisters, whatever is true,
> whatever is noble, whatever is right, whatever is pure,
> whatever is lovely, whatever is admirable—if anything
> is excellent or praiseworthy—think about such things.
>
> PHILIPPIANS 4:8

Should You Share Your Sexual Fantasy?

Perhaps you've heard something, read something, or merely imagined something that arouses your sexual senses and gets your engine humming. In your dream world, you'd do that very thing, and it would bring mind-blowing pleasure. Should you share that sexual fantasy with your husband?

I'm all for honesty in marriage, but I don't think honesty involves sharing every single thought that crosses your mind. Husbands often figure this out before wives do, when they learn how to answer the question, "Does this make me look fat?" Indeed, the Bible tells us not to lie, but also to be careful what we say and how we say it. "Watch your tongue and keep your mouth shut, and you will stay out of trouble" (Proverbs 21:23 NLT). Titus 3:2 advises us "to speak evil of no one, to avoid quarreling, to be gentle, and to show perfect courtesy toward all people" (ESV).

We have a choice whether to volunteer to our mates the sexual thoughts that creep into our minds. So what should be the standard for whether we tell our spouses our sexual fantasies? Here are some things to consider.

Does it involve third persons? Oftentimes, we think third persons applies merely to adultery, threesomes, or voyeurism. These are obviously off limits. However, third persons should not be allowed in your visual or thought life either. Watching pornography is inviting people outside of your marriage to arouse you sexually or demonstrate acts for you to copy. Reading erotica and calling to mind fictional characters to become titillated is another way of getting third parties involved.

Focus your sexual energy on your husband—both in practice and, as much as possible, in thought. Jesus said that looking at another lustfully rises to the level of adultery (Matthew 5:28). We'll likely notice attractive people in our midst. We're married, not dead. But dwelling on the appearance of, or our desire for, another person becomes infidelity. We are taking sexual energy that rightfully belongs to our mates and transferring it to another.

If your sexual fantasy involves a third person, it's not one you want to share. In fact, it's a fantasy you should shove out of your mind when it crops up. Come up with another fantasy—one that involves you and your mate exclusively.

Does it violate biblical commands about sexuality? There are prohibitions against certain sexual activities in the Bible, including adultery, bestiality, incest, and other extremes. So obviously, no animals, right? (See Exodus 22:19.) But also no injury or degradation. These are not in keeping with the biblical commands for husbands to "love their wives as their own bodies" or for a wife to "respect her husband" (see Ephesians 5:25–33).

Remember the principles of kindness, respect, love, and gentleness in Scripture (see Galatians 5:22–23 and Ephesians 5:21–33). Whatever you do in the bedroom should not rise to the level of sinfulness but should aim for the ideal of 1 Corinthians 13 love.

Consider whether you'd be asking for something that does not honor your husband and God. If so, it's not a fantasy you want to share or act out. God is in favor of sexuality, including adventurous activities (read Song of Songs for confirmation), but even in the bedroom, we should be treating each other with love and care.

Is it based on something you did with someone else? If you were sexually active with someone before you married your husband, there will be some repeat activities. But comparisons are a no-no, as are efforts to re-create a special memory from a previous sexual relationship. What if you liked the way Mr. X did that one little thing eight years ago, and you wish you could do that again? Let it go.

Don't try to make your husband be like someone you knew before. Create new memories. Think of how your man can delight you in fresh and meaningful ways. Focus your sexual energy on your here-and-now hubby.

Are you demanding that your mate fulfill your fantasy? You might desire something that's perfectly fine—like an unusual location or a particular sexy outfit or a new sexual activity. However, if you're expecting to share your fantasy and demand on the spot that your hubby meet it, take a step back. This is your sexual fantasy, not his.

You don't have a right to demand something outside of his comfort zone and throw a fit if he doesn't line up with your imagination. Indeed, you have a right to expect sexual intimacy (1 Corinthians 7:3–5), but "extra" stuff is up for discussion, not demand. Your attitude, even in the bedroom, should be like that of Christ Jesus: "Do nothing out of selfish ambition or vain conceit. Rather, in humility value others above yourselves, not looking to your own interests but each of you to the interests of the others" (Philippians 2:3–4).

If you take a loving attitude, and your request is not something sinful, you might find that over time, your hubby comes around and is willing to give it a try. If so, your fantasy fulfilled will be even better because he'll be "all in" and excited about the experience as well.

Are you ready to hear his fantasy? If you want him to listen to yours, you have to be willing to listen to his. You might absolutely love whatever idea he throws out, or you might cringe and think, "Holy heart palpitations, I could never do that!"

But it's only fair that you hear each other out. You don't have to kowtow to his fantasy, but you shouldn't insult him for thinking of it. The idea that, for example, he wants to lay you out on your parents' kitchen table and make you scream until the ceiling chandelier breaks shouldn't result in you declaring you can't believe he would think that, and how are you supposed to go to Thanksgiving dinner with your parents knowing he wants to do that to you, and how can you ever sit at their table while thinking about how he'd like to move that basted turkey out of the way and baste you with sex juices instead!

You're not required to do whatever his fantasy is, but listen to it, consider what about it might appeal to him, and decide whether it's something you would be willing to do or to suggest a tweaked version.

Should You Go Along with His Sexual Fantasy?

How do you decide whether to go along with his sexual fantasy? Many of the same questions apply here as in the previous section. But here are some more guidelines on whether to act out a sexual fantasy together.

Does it remind him of pornography? One question wives have asked is: "Hubby wants to do X, which he saw in porn. Should I do it?" I don't believe that anything and everything in porn is off the table; after all, porn shows intercourse, and that's clearly on God's go-to-town list. To my mind, the concern appears when performing a sexual action taps into pornography. The issue is not whether the fantasy could be found in porn, but whether it brings to mind someone else. If it does, come up with a new fantasy and create memories all your own.

Is it painful rather than pleasurable? One of the expectations of sex in marriage is that it will feel good. If it doesn't, something is amiss. Usually, people want to experience pleasure and try to avoid pain. Yet sometimes a spouse confuses the two.

Here's one explanation for why pain in the bedroom might

appeal to some. Pain can bring your attention to a localized body part. The body's response to pain is to release natural opioids, such as endorphins, to combat the discomfort. Friction in the injured area (like when you rub a stubbed toe) can also relieve pain. The juxtaposition of these sensations, coupled with arousal, can cause people to link pain and pleasure. There's more to it than that, but I don't need to get into that here.

The Bible never indicates that pain should be part of sexual intimacy in marriage. The Song of Songs communicates tenderness between the two lovers. Deuteronomy 24:5 says that a newlywed man should "be free to stay at home and bring happiness to the wife he has married." Genesis 2:24 says that the two become "one flesh."

Ephesians 5:28–31 is clear about how we should approach our spouses' bodies:

> Husbands ought to love their wives as their own bodies. He who loves his wife loves himself. After all, no one ever hated their own body, but they feed and care for their body, just as Christ does the church—for we are members of his body. "For this reason a man will leave his father and mother and be united to his wife, and the two will become one flesh."

Your spouse should not put you in physical pain for his arousal, nor should you put him in physical pain for yours.*

Does it compromise others? Having sex in public places, where there is a high likelihood of being seen by someone else,

* Prior sexual abuse can complicate this issue. Previous victims may not be able to participate in something that reminds them of the horrendous experience they endured. Professional help may be needed to work through what's normal, what's not, and how you can successfully approach sex with your spouse.

may heighten your arousal. I understand the rush of danger pulsing through your veins, but it's not fair to assault someone's eyes by making them view you and your husband mid-coitus. In addition to treating your spouse with respect, respect others and keep your sexuality private between the two of you.

Does it gross you out? Okay, yeah, this isn't so straightforward. But really, some stuff is just off limits because it's totally icky to you. If you have a good sexual relationship with your husband, you should be able to say sometimes, "No, not that." It's never okay to demand or force your spouse to perform sexual acts with or for you that are utterly repulsive to them. (If biblically mandated intercourse is repulsive, there are serious underlying issues that need addressing.)

Degrading your mate in the bedroom is not God's design for sexual intimacy. So if the thought of engaging in your husband's fantasy grosses you out, ask yourself why. You might be able to try something out of the ordinary after all. But if your stomach is still twisting like a tornado, you can opt out, as long as you are putting your full effort into participating in your sex life within marriage and satisfying your husband sexually.

What do you do when you don't want to go along? Start by praying. If the fantasy is not clearly unbiblical to you, ask for God's wisdom on whether you should oblige or pass. Then open up a conversation with your husband (outside the bedroom) about what you want your sex life to look like. Reassure him that you desire him sexually and want to experience satisfaction and intimacy. Gently explain your reservations and reasons for not wanting to indulge the fantasy.

If he continues to demand or cajole, set boundaries. Be reasonable and respectful, yet firm. Your body belongs to him, but it belongs to you as well.

Married, Consenting Adults: Whose Okay Really Matters?

Have you noticed that a number of historically problematic sexual activities have become No Big Deal or are even encouraged? Most often, the reason I hear is that it's between "consenting adults."

We also hear this about marriage. After all, whose business is it if a married couple mutually agrees to engage in whatever sexual act they choose? They're adults. They consented. Surely, then, everything's okay.

This trend in the general culture is disturbing, but among Christians, it's particularly distressing. Even if husband and wife consent, another vote matters! Do you have the consent of your Lord and Father, the one who created sex?

What if you decide you want your husband to get his sexual needs met elsewhere? Or you're both willing to couple swap, or "swing"? Our Lord says:

> "You must not commit adultery" (Exodus 20:14; Deuteronomy 5:18 NLT).
>
> "You must not covet your neighbor's wife" (Exodus 20:17 NLT).
>
> "The man who commits adultery is an utter fool, for he destroys himself" (Proverbs 6:32 NLT).
>
> "Marriage should be honored by all, and the marriage bed kept pure, for God will judge the adulterer and all the sexually immoral" (Hebrews 13:4).

How about watching porn, reading erotica, going to strip joints together? After all, you're consenting to do it together. What if it's just to spice up your marriage?

> I made a covenant with my eyes
> not to look lustfully at a young woman.
> For what is our lot from God above,
> our heritage from the Almighty on high?
> Is it not ruin for the wicked,
> disaster for those who do wrong?
> Does he not see my ways
> and count my every step? (Job 31:1–4)

> I tell you that anyone who looks at a woman lustfully has already committed adultery with her in his heart. (Matthew 5:28)

> Put to death, therefore, whatever belongs to your earthly nature: sexual immorality, impurity, lust, evil desires and greed, which is idolatry. (Colossians 3:5)

Maybe you get aroused by striking your mate in the bedroom, by introducing intense S&M practices, by pushing your pain-pleasure limits? Isn't it okay if you're both consenting?

> The Lord examines the righteous, but the wicked, those who love violence, he hates with a passion. (Psalm 11:5)

> From the fruit of their lips people enjoy good things, but the unfaithful have an appetite for violence. (Proverbs 13:2)

> As God's chosen people, holy and dearly loved, clothe yourselves with compassion, kindness, humility, gentleness and patience. (Colossians 3:12)

> You have been called to live in freedom, my brothers and sisters. But don't use your freedom to satisfy your sinful

> nature. Instead, use your freedom to serve one another in love. (Galatians 5:13 NLT)
>
> The Holy Spirit produces this kind of fruit in our lives: love, joy, peace, patience, kindness, goodness, faithfulness, gentleness, and self-control. There is no law against these things! (Galatians 5:22–23 NLT)

When you consider what sexual intimacy in your marriage should look like, think not only about the husband's consent and the wife's consent, but the consent of the third partner in your marriage—God Himself. Indeed, I would argue that God's consent matters the most.

Chapter 11
EXPERIENCING AN ORGASM

This might be one of the most frequently asked questions about sex: "How do I reach that pinnacle of sexual satisfaction?" It's certainly the subject of plenty of women's magazine articles. Have you browsed the newsstand lately?

It is true that you will likely enjoy and desire sex more if you can—at least sometimes—experience the physical ecstasy we call "orgasm."

> Eat, friends, and drink;
> drink your fill of love.
>
> Song of Songs 5:1

How to Orgasm

Have you had an orgasm? It's an experience many wives desire but struggle to achieve. It doesn't come easily to everyone. Here are some tips for getting there.

Don't try to orgasm. Yes, it's a worthy goal, and I'm in favor of reaching that awe-inducing climax and yelling "Yippee!" at its apex. However, trying to attain an orgasm is like looking for the perfect shoes. You almost never find them when you're out hunting down what to wear with that outfit you paid too much for. But go out browsing with a girlfriend to enjoy the fun of shopping, and *voila!* There they are—the perfect shoes, practically winking at you through the display window.

Likewise, orgasms are not what you should aim for. Aim instead for pleasure, pleasure, and more pleasure. When the pleasure becomes particularly intense, orgasm occurs. So your target should be enjoying the sex as much as you possibly can.

Learn about your body. Read up on the anatomy of the female body. Learn the parts that constitute arousal areas and how they work. The most thorough treatment I've read was from *Intended for Pleasure* by Ed and Gaye Wheat, but there are other sources. One important fact is that the clitoris is where orgasm occurs for women, and this body part appears to have no other purpose than inducing sexual arousal. (Thank You, God.) The Wheats state that "sufficient physical stimulation of the clitoris alone will produce orgasm in nearly all women."[16] Of course, what constitutes "sufficient physical stimulation" is what wives, and husbands, need to know.

Some experts suggest experimenting with your own body, discovering where you like to be touched and with what intensity. It will feel different with your own hand versus your husband's, but this information can be valuable. You can even make this part of a lovemaking session. Most husbands are very aroused by their wives touching themselves, and this can become part of foreplay. It can help him to see what you like.

You can also have your husband explore your body. For this session, I suggest the wife remove her clothing but the husband remain dressed. (It can be awfully hard for him to not rush in to penetration if he's already naked.) Dedicate at least fifteen minutes, but even better a half hour, to him touching you with his hands and lips. It may feel selfish to indulge only one of you, but learning what causes arousal for the wife will also benefit the husband in the long run.

Slow way down. Men typically do not require as much foreplay as women. In fact, husbands have been compared to microwaves and wives to slow cookers for how long it takes them to heat up. It takes some time for most women to become aroused and fully lubricated, and for the inner vagina lips (labia minora) to swell.

Moreover, women are mental multitaskers. This can be a problem when it comes to sex. It takes time to wind down and push the to-do list to the back of our minds. To swat away those pesky distractions rushing through our brains. To relax into the arms of our beloved. To feel valued, treasured, and loved in that moment. To let go and surrender to the sensations our bodies are experiencing.

It can be a good thing when the lovemaking experience is slowed down. It ensures that a couple basks in the delights of each other. Give yourself time for pleasure and intensity to build.

Focus on the sensations. The female orgasm is mostly mental. Too often we think about *sex and*… For example, sex and your shopping list, sex and the lyrics to the song on the radio, sex and the way your breasts sag to the side instead of perking up like you wish they would. Instead, focus on what's happening to your body. Give in to it. Enjoy it.

Make your pleasure almost like meditation. Train yourself to focus on where your husband is touching, kissing, or fondling you. Think intently about your private areas as your husband pleasures them. If stray thoughts come in (and they likely will), return your mental attention to your body and the stimulation of your five senses.

Most women must practice this level of concentration. It may take time to do it with ease.

Communicate. Tell your husband what you like. When something feels particularly good, let him know to keep doing it, or have him increase the intensity. When adjustments need to be made, verbally suggest what you want or direct his hands or lips to the area you want aroused.

Can this be awkward? Um, yeah. I've never seen a Hollywood love scene where one actor said to the other, "Oh, not there. Over a little bit. Yeah, that's it."

Two things to remember: (1) He wants to pleasure you, so if something else would do more to rev up your engine, he wants to know; (2) He'll respond much better to positive feedback than critical reviews of his performance. For example, rather than saying, "That doesn't feel good," move his hand and say, "I love it when you touch me *there*." Smiles, oohs, aahs, and groans also let a hubby know when he's hit the jackpot. You could throw in a "You rock my world, baby!" if you feel moved. That usually goes over well.

Surrender to the moment. Orgasm is a paradox of tension and letting go. When a woman feels extreme sexual arousal, her body tenses. But she must surrender to the pleasurable sensations in order for her body to climax. This is something you might need to practice. When you start feeling intense pleasure, concentrate on the body part being aroused and relax it. Do this a few times and see if your pleasure increases.

Give in to the moment when it arrives. Make noises. Grimace. Scream. Flail about. Whatever floats your boat. I wonder about couples who videotape their lovemaking sessions because I'm pretty sure that orgasms are not pretty. If you watched a woman undergoing an intense orgasm, she might look like a rabid animal. However, this is not the time to worry about how you look or what the neighbors might think if they heard you. (They're probably thinking "Good for her!") At that apex of pleasure, let go and revel in your one-fleshness.

Multiple and Simultaneous Orgasms

If you currently have orgasms and want to increase the intensity even more, you might be able to achieve multiple and/or simultaneous orgasms. Having multiple orgasms is enjoyable for you and also delights your husband. And achieving climax together can be a breathtaking, intimate moment for the two of you. But the question is *how*?

Multiple Orgasms. First of all, it isn't a myth. Quite a few women experience multiple orgasms in a single sexual encounter.

The easiest orgasm to achieve is purely clitoral—your husband stimulates your clitoris to the point of intense pleasure and eventually that tension releases as a physical wave of spasms and a mental *holy-shivers-that-feels-good* recognition. You know you have had an orgasm when you feel your vagina squeeze and release and your eyes roll to the back of your head and fall onto your pillow. (You can pick them up and return them to your sockets later.)

Women can also have a vaginal orgasm, which typically occurs with penetration. This orgasm feels less frenetic and deeper but it may last longer. Some experts believe the key factor for a vaginal orgasm is contact with the G-spot.* I'm not sure that's a must. The clitoris is still involved in this orgasm, because it receives indirect pressure through thrusting.

* The Grafenberg Spot, or G-spot, is an erogenous zone located on the inner wall of the vagina.

Given that not all orgasms are the same, not all multiple orgasms feel the same. You may have more than one clitoral orgasm, a clitoral and a vaginal, more than one vaginal, and they will all feel different. Clitoral orgasms also range in their intensity, contractions, feeling of sparks or waves, etc. Which is awesome! We wives can experience a variety of orgasmic experiences; meanwhile, a husband's climaxes may be fabulous but they're all pretty straightforward.

As for how to, here are some tips.

Slow, fast, climax, slow, fast, climax, repeat. With clitoral orgasms especially, you can make it a loop. Typically, wives want husbands to go slow for a while and then quicken the pace and increase the pressure. Once a wife has reached the pinnacle of pleasure and achieved orgasm, hubby needs to back down on the pace and pressure. He doesn't need to start over, but since the wife has fallen down the hump in excitement level, she needs to be built up again to reach another climax.

Think of it like a roller coaster. The ride inches slowly up to that first peak, and then you go careening down the hill with a huge grin and a scream, and then the next hill comes. You have to get up that hill again, and you lose a little speed doing so. But when you go down that second hill, you're screaming again (*Yippee, this is fun!*). It's slow, fast, slow, fast—or, if you prefer, up, down, up, down.

Clitoral stimulation, then vaginal. Even though a wife can have more than one vaginal orgasm, the clitoral is easier for most women to reach. I suggest focusing on getting there first, then having the husband enter.

To get that second (or ninth) orgasm, you can do a few things:

Play with sexual positioning. I'm not talking about some contortionist act. Just tilt your hips, raise your legs, try woman-on-top, use the edge of the bed get into an angle that arouses you more or provides deeper penetration. You get the idea.

Have him stimulate other areas of your body. If your breasts are erogenous zones, or him kissing your neck makes you go crazy, add that extra attention to see if that gets you over the brink.

Continue to stimulate the clitoris while hubby is inside. He can do this with his fingers or, if you are comfortable, you can do it yourself. You could also go for a succession of clitoral orgasms and wait on the intercourse. Make that decision together to see what you want to do.

If at first you don't succeed ... Don't sweat it. Think of sex without an orgasm as being like a brownie. Sex with an orgasm is a brownie with a dollop of ice cream. Sex with multiple orgasms adds chocolate sauce. Believe me, if you offer me a brownie and ice cream, but you don't have Hershey's syrup in your cabinet, I'm still going to enjoy every bite.

If you don't get wave after wave of awesome orgasm on your first (or fifth) try, keep making love! Try something a little different. Communicate. Experiment. Have fun with it. Ultimately, the best way to know what turns you on the most is not for me to draw a diagram or write an instruction manual (*ignore the irony*), but for you and your husband to explore each other's bodies and sexual responses.

Simultaneous Orgasm. Reaching orgasm together can be a wonderful experience. Here are my thoughts on that serendipity.

Timing. For each of you to reach climax at the same time, you simply have to figure out who needs to hold off until the other spouse gets there. One of you must come close, have patience while the other gets close, and then knock yourselves out.

The ideal simultaneous orgasm is with penetration. It may be easier for some women to have a clitoral orgasm beforehand

and then have their husbands enter and bring them to climax again. Unlike the guys, we gals can handle a two-fer, and the first orgasm may help get a wife to a sexual plateau where it isn't that hard to vault up again into orgasmic pleasure.

Once you both get close, one of you having an orgasm will likely help the other get there. The spasms of a wife's orgasm provide pressure on her husband's penis to bring about ejaculation. And the husband's ejaculation will likely cause him to thrust deeper, thus contacting sensitive spots inside a woman that may respond with orgasm.

Luck. You can do some planning with this, but getting two people to climax together is a bit like trying to get two runners to cross the finish line at the same moment. You can try your best to match another's stride, but breaking that tape together would be difficult to achieve consistently. So take it when it happens, but as a friend of mine said, "This isn't synchronized swimming."

Experience. Couples are better able to climax together when they are older and have been together longer. Why? It's relatively difficult for a young man to postpone climax, while an older man can usually control his climax better. Additionally, over time sexually active married couples learn to gauge each other's physical responses and adjust accordingly.

At this point in my marriage, neither of us has to say, "I'm almost there," because the other spouse can tell. We've been there enough to know.

That doesn't mean the young'uns can't get it. But if you haven't experienced it yet, you may in the future.

Have fun trying. Most women will achieve multiple and simultaneous orgasms at some point in their marriage. However, from my experience and talking with other wives who have had multiple and simultaneous orgasms, the most enjoyable sex comes not from meeting such goals but from having physical, emotional, and spiritual intimacy in the bedroom. Seeking these higher goals, in turn, helps you reach the physical ones. Feeling comfortable and confident sexually with your husband, being able to explore and communicate with each other during sex, and each of you having the attitude of pleasuring the other will go a long way toward experiencing multiple and simultaneous orgasms.

Why I Sometimes Don't Care about the Orgasm

While some wives want to experience orgasm every time they have sex, a good number of us are okay with forgoing the peak of all peaks. Why would you be willing to pass up the orgasm every so often? Maybe you can relate to some of these reasons:

You get it almost every time. Orgasm isn't an issue for you because you enjoy it on a frequent basis—maybe even multiple orgasms. Since you and your husband make this a regular priority, you have no doubt you can achieve orgasm the next time. Thus, skipping an orgasm now and then isn't a big deal.

You want to focus on your husband's pleasure. You like putting your husband first and foremost at times. Most of your lovemaking is equally satisfying for both of you, but you see the value in concentrating on one spouse sometimes (Philippians 2:4). And this time, you want to put your whole focus on his fulfillment, not worrying too much about your own. If you climax, fine. If not, you can go without this time.

Your body isn't cooperating. For reasons known or unknown, your body simply isn't responding the way it usually does. Maybe it's an off-kilter time of the month or you're recovering from an illness or have piled-up stress or physical fatigue. Whatever the cause, you're happy to engage in physical intimacy, but reaching orgasm requires more effort than you want to give at that moment. It's enough to simply enjoy the closeness with your husband.

You're concentrating on other sensations. Climax is amazing. Really, really amazing. But other sensations in sex are pleasurable as well. Maybe you're simply enjoying the loving caresses from your husband's hands or the tenderness of his lips as he kisses you all over. Perhaps you're reveling in the gentle friction and pressure of your husband's manhood inside you, astounded at how well your bodies fit together to create that one-flesh experience (Genesis 2:24). Whatever it is that feels so good, this time it feels like enough—climax optional.

You don't have time. You and hubby have squeezed a sexual encounter into an already full schedule or sneaked away from the children for what you know will be a short-lived opportunity. It's quickie time. While you might want an orgasm, it's not necessarily achievable in the time you have. So you can take it or leave it, still feeling good that you two engaged in sexual intimacy—be it ever so hurried.

If a wife never desires an orgasm or if she never has one (no matter how much she desires it), some red flags should go up. Husbands almost always climax through sex, but wives often require a more gentle and more guided touch. Orgasm is not the be-all and end-all, but it's a worthwhile goal for the vast majority of sexual encounters. God designed women to orgasm through clitoral and vaginal stimulation, and that beautiful sexual symphony should be heard often in marriage.

Yet, if you don't desire the orgasm every now and then, you're not weird or broken. Sometimes we wives can pass on it and be perfectly happy.

What's So Great about an Orgasm?

Why should you even want an orgasm? Here's some of what makes this experience so great.

Your pleasure. To reach orgasm, most couples must be intentional about it. A few wives orgasm easily, but for most, a sliver of foreplay immediately followed by intercourse ain't gonna cut it. Which means if she orgasms, the couple has placed a priority on her pleasure as well as his.

In many cases, the husband is demonstrating a desire to arouse, excite, and satisfy his wife—even when it means sex takes longer than required for his own satisfaction. A wife's orgasm shows intention and priority placed on making sure both partners experience a peak of pleasure in the marriage bed.

Health. Research studies have long shown health benefits of sex and, more specifically, orgasm. Several of these benefits, we wives can personally confirm. Orgasm produces a flow of the bonding chemical oxytocin, which produces feelings of connection and calm—the same feelings that help you get a good night's sleep. Endorphins produced during orgasm increase pain tolerance, thus alleviating headache or backache or even cramps. Blood flow in the brain is increased, keeping your noggin healthy. Regular orgasms give a workout to the muscles responsible for maintaining continence, muscles that weaken with age and could use some exercise.

Orgasms have also been linked to lower blood pressure and reduced anxiety and depression, as well as giving a more youthful appearance. While some of these benefits result from sex itself, orgasms seem to boost the positive effects.

Mental break. To the awe or confusion of most men, women's brains are inundated with a thousand thoughts. At any given moment, ask me what I'm thinking, and you might get up to fifteen items that have passed through my head in the last three seconds. I'm telling you, it's a mine field in there.

However, in the middle of a fabulous orgasm, all those tangled thoughts and constant concerns melt away. A woman's brain is overloaded with an explosion of pleasure—resulting in a lovely mental respite, a Zen-like moment. Your body releases tension, and a treasured calm washes over you.

God's beautiful design. When God created people and marriage, He had innumerable choices of how to design the sexual act. Look around at the rest of nature, and you can see some of the options. When it came to His people, though, He seemed to have really thought it through. Considering His design, the orgasm is one part of an amazing way to link a husband and wife in sexual intercourse.

When a wife's arousal increases, she tends to desire more frequent thrusting and deeper penetration. When a husband thrusts more frequently and penetrates more deeply, more sensitive areas of her vagina are contacted, thus increasing her excitement even more. When her husband closes in on his climax, his penis pulses with the release of ejaculate. When the wife closes in on climax, her vagina contracts with spasms. Both of these actions encourage the other's completion and sensations of pleasure. It's a dance of body parts, each doing their thing, but interwoven in a rather astounding way. Her climax facilitates his, and his climax facilitates hers. What a beautiful design.

Does this happen every time? No. But part of God's setup here is a lifetime together to learn each other's bodies and godly attitudes that make it far more likely for both of you to enjoy sex and experience climax. The longer you're married, the more you attend to each other's pleasure, the more you live out God's intended plan, and the more likely you are to perfect the dance. You get the steps down, you feel each other's rhythm, you synchronize your movements, and you almost move as one.

For these and other reasons, orgasms are a wonderful addition to the sexual experience, and one worth aiming for.

But I Still Can't Orgasm!

No matter how many tips I give, there are wives out there who say, "But I still can't orgasm!"

Some women feel they have tried every piece of advice they've been offered or could seek out on their own, and the much-touted climax still dangles out of reach. If this is you, perhaps there's an underlying problem getting in the way of your ability to achieve the Big O. Let's cover a few possibilities.

Pain. How can you feel extreme pleasure when sex flat-out hurts? If you've been hoping that having an orgasm will deal with the pain you've been experiencing, that's not likely to work. You need to address the pain itself, so you can enjoy sex with your husband. Then you'll be able to feel the full pleasure of sexual intimacy and eventually reach climax.

If sex hurts, talk to your doctor about solutions. There is likely something that can be done to address your discomfort. Don't settle for having pain during sex. It isn't supposed to hurt, so treat it like any other pain in your body and look for answers and treatment. Be sure to read the section on Addressing Physical Pain—What to Do When Sex Is Painful.

Insensitivity. Some wives have reduced sensitivity. They feel pleasure, but it's not quite enough to get them over the hump to orgasm. What are some possible reasons? Oftentimes, medications are at play. Certain medications, including some antidepressants and oral contraceptives, have been known to make it more difficult to achieve climax.

Talk to your doctor and consider alternatives. You might want to try another antidepressant or a different contraception method.

Scar tissue could also be a factor. Your gynecologist might have some suggestions for getting past that obstacle.

Psychological barriers. Even though you feel like you've done everything reasonable, you could still have psychological barriers keeping you from achieving orgasm. For instance, the wife who can't surrender entirely because she was falsely taught that good girls don't enjoy sex that much. The woman who was molested or raped and has buried memories of that horrible abuse. The wife who reconciled with a cheating husband and wants deep intimacy but struggles with trust in the marriage bed.

Reaching the peak of sexual pleasure requires being able to surrender to the experience, and a bad sexual history can interfere with feeling comfortable and confident about letting go. If you believe something in your past is interfering with your getting the full pleasure God desires you to have in marital intimacy, speak with your husband, a friend, a mentor, your pastor, and/or a counselor. Don't stop looking for help and answers.

Fatigue. Too pooped to pop? There is a certain amount of energy required to reach climax. If you are super-low on sleep, not eating well, stressed beyond belief, depressed, or deficient in vitamins, you might find yourself struggling to march all the way up that hill of happiness to the peak of ecstasy.

Do what you know you should be doing. Sleep. Eat well. Rest. Get a checkup. Stay healthy. Be good to yourself outside the bedroom so you can feel good inside the bedroom.

Figure out what's preventing you from achieving orgasm,

then address it. With effort and time, you may find yourself finally enjoying that peak of pleasure.

Five Tips for Reaching Climax

Summing up this section on Experiencing an Orgasm, here are five quick tips for reaching climax.

Empty your brain. Okay, that may have made you clutch your sides with laughter. The notion of a wife, mom, household manager, worker, and taskmaster shoving everything out of her brain is like suggesting you lasso a hurricane. But get your rope ready, girlfriend, because I believe in you!

As long as you have other things running through your brain besides your arousal and love and connection, it will be hard to climax. How do you "empty your brain"? Start by preparing for sex, doing what you need to do to focus on the marriage bed. Then shift your mind away from stray thoughts that try to pull you away and focus on what's happening in your body and with your husband. Meditate on the sensations in your body and lean into your pleasure. This is a process you'll likely have to practice.

By the way, one of those distractions you don't want running through your brain is concern about whether or not you'll climax. Thinking about pleasure and thinking about climax aren't the same thing. Focus on your feelings, then let the excitement happen.

Get to know your body. In one sense, female orgasm is pretty straightforward. Stimulation of the clitoris, direct or indirect, leads to that *Squeee!* moment. But how your clitoris likes to be stimulated is specific to you.

So to achieve orgasm, you need to experiment and explore how you like to be touched. Some wives like to try a bit of this on their own first, as personal education, so they can better instruct their husbands later. Or a husband can try a bunch of different touches—varying pressure, stroke, angle, location, etc. You can also work together, with you touching yourself and letting him mimic the motions.

It could be well worth your time to take a lovemaking session, or two or three, and find out what really gets you revved up. Your husband may be willing to give this a go if you let him know you want to increase your excitement in the bedroom. During this time, don't focus so much on climax as learning what gives you extreme pleasure. Extreme pleasure should eventually lead to climax.

Ask for what you want. If it feels awkward to speak up for something you want during sex, raise your hand. I see you out there! And years ago I would have raised my hand too. But honestly, how's a guy to know what feels bad or good to you unless you tell him?

If you really want your husband to stop that "*Good heavens, doesn't he know I hate that?*" move, you have to speak up. Of course, you should use your nice words—something like, "That's a little too much pressure for me. Could you touch me more gently? I think that would really turn me on."

When your husband really hits the sweet spot, let him know. Cheer him on, as if that man just shot a nothing-but-net basket. (*You go, hubby! Well done.*) You can leave out your pom-poms (or not), but tell him with words, moans, happy noises, or a little mutual pleasuring when he's doing something that arouses you.

Change it up. Even when something feels totally awesome at the moment, you may need something else a minute later to keep you rising toward that peak. I feel for husbands, because some of them treat their wives' lady parts like a genie lamp—thinking once they find the right place and way to rub, they can simply keep doing it and the magic will be released.

It's more like *rub a little here, rub a little there, harder here, softer there*—like a moving target at times. But hey, your fabulous hubby is up to the challenge, and you can let him know what your body is craving. Help him vary his approach and keep you on the path toward the peak.

As your excitement increases, you'll likely want greater pressure, faster stroking, and maybe additional stimulation elsewhere—such as touching or kissing your breasts or digital penetration. If your arousal reaches a plateau, change something up and see if that gets you climbing again.

Fogettaboutit! Worry tenses your body and makes you less responsive to arousal. So once you're in the midst of sexual pleasure, simply enjoy it. Get as much pleasure as you can from the experience. And be sure to pleasure your husband as well. Your ultimate goal is intimacy, and climax is only one thing that contributes to that one-flesh experience.

If you don't get there today, you might get there tomorrow. Or next week. Or while at the in-laws' house during the holidays. (Wouldn't that be a hoot?) But focus on your lovemaking feeling fabulous, and you may find the orgasm comes on its own.

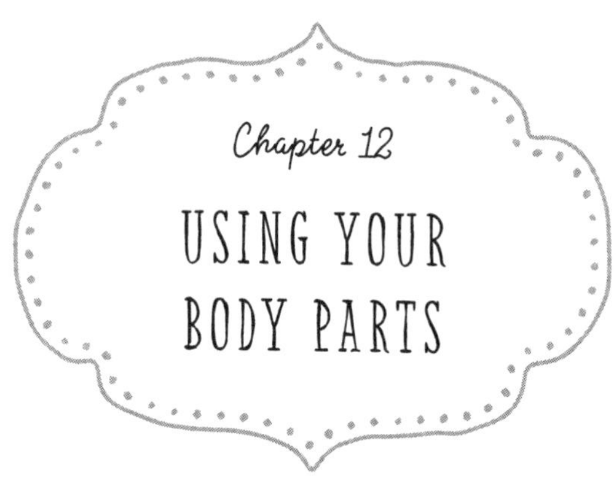

Chapter 12
USING YOUR BODY PARTS

Sex should involve most of our bodies as we touch, kiss, and join together in this intimate act to express and foster love. So let's discuss how to use your various body parts in lovemaking.

> The wife does not have authority over her own body but yields it to her husband. In the same way, the husband does not have authority over his own body but yields it to his wife.
>
> 1 Corinthians 7:4

First, Your Mind

When it comes to using your body for marital intimacy, let's cover first things first. While some husbands might assert that sex begins somewhere between your belt buckle and your kneecaps, we wives know sex begins in the mind. That's the body part we ladies need to get into the groove so we can … well, get into the groove.

Unfortunately, we mental multitaskers often have difficulty focusing on sexual intimacy with our husbands. It might not seem like such a tall order, but setting aside all the other thoughts and concentrating solely and wholly on lovemaking can be a challenge for many of us.

How can we involve our minds in sexual intimacy?

Set aside the time and space. Start by making sure external distractions are not competing. Yes, there are times when you must squeeze sex into eight minutes flat while your toddler is finishing his nap or you shove work piles from the bed to make love, but that shouldn't be the norm.

Set aside time on your calendar or in your schedule. Make it a priority somewhere below breathing or eating and way above a pedicure or polishing faucet fixtures. When you set your mind to spending the next thirty minutes in physical intimacy with your husband, you can more freely engage without thinking of everything else you could be doing.

Also set aside space so you two have room to make love without the distractions of children's toys, electronics, to-do lists, etc. Remove from your sight whatever might compete for your attention.

Start anticipating in advance. Think ahead of time about how you will feel in the arms of your beloved. Be positive in your anticipation—considering how your senses will be awakened, how your husband's touch will comfort and arouse you, how you want to pleasure him and be pleasured, how precious this gift of sexual union is.

Some wives anticipate sex with dread, ranking it alongside toilet cleaning in their daily task list. If you experience pain or have no drive, you need to address that issue. Yet our brains are very powerful, so if you simply don't look forward to the experience, retrain your mind. Choose to focus your mental energy on those lovemaking moments that were enjoyable and anticipate having that pleasure once again. The more you joyfully approach an event, the more likely you are to enjoy it.

Focus on your hubby. See that hottie over there? Yep, that one: your hubby. That's the guy you chose (and who chose you). You must've thought he was something special when you said "I do," so dwell on what's so great about your husband.

Think about the physical and internal attributes that are attractive to you. Drop the negative stuff from your mind. Of course, he's annoying at times; my husband is too. (Guess what? We annoy them back.) This is the time to pull your mind toward the beauty of his body, the strength of his character, the fun he brings to life, the gift of his love.

Consider how you desire your husband and how you want him to rejoice in you and be captivated by your love (Proverbs 5:18–19). Keep your mind actively engaged in thinking about your husband and lover.

Become aware of your own body. Your body is equipped with five incredible senses and an amazing number of skin receptors that register touch, temperature, vibration, pressure, and more. On top of that, God blessed certain parts of your body with extra sensitivity to respond happily to sexual arousal.

When making love with your husband, turn your mind to the sensations your body is experiencing. Think about the places he touches, kisses, fondles, strokes, penetrates. If your mind begins to wander to whether you turned off the oven or how much you distrust congress or when you last had a pedicure, regain control and return your mind to where it should be—on the interesting tickles and tingles of your body.

Also think about how you can produce delightful feelings for your husband. Your hands, lips, breasts, and other parts of your body have the amazing ability to bring him great pleasure.

Turn your mind to gratitude. Gratitude is an attitude nurtured in the mind. God has given married couples the gift of sexual intimacy. He could have made it simply for reproduction, but our Father wanted us to enjoy sex and use it to grow intimacy. What a gift!

Just as you pause to soak in the beauty of a colorful sunset or the melodious sounds of your favorite song, pause in your mind to be grateful for sexual intimacy. Make it a regular habit to thank God and your mate for your sexual pleasure.

Begin with the mind, and then embark on the wonderful journey of your bodies coming together in marital intimacy.

What to Do with Your Hands

Did you know that if you type the keyword *hands* into a Bible search engine, you'll get 579 results. *Hand*, 748 results. But *touch*? Only 40.

I scanned every one of those 1,367 verses, with help from the Holy Spirit and caffeine, to see what the Bible had to say about those things in connection to sex. There wasn't much. Well, except for Zephaniah 3:16: "Do not let your hands hang limp." Just kidding. That verse has nothing to do with sex (even if it is good advice).

Yet hands represent several important concepts in the Bible, such as:

possession (e.g., one nation given into the hands of another)
power (e.g., David's hand killing Goliath)
skill (e.g., the work of one's hands)
presence (e.g., God's hand with someone)
reverence (e.g., lifting hands in prayer)

importance (e.g., sitting at one's right hand)
tenderness (e.g., Jesus touching those He healed)

All of these could apply to marriage. For example, the only one who gets to put hands on our girly parts is the hubster. (Okay, gynecologists too, but let's not digress to the uncomfortable memory of your last Pap smear.) The point is, my hubby and I put our hands on each other because "My beloved is mine and I am his" (Song of Songs 2:16). Possession.

We can also convey power, skill, presence, reverence (for the Creator of the human body), importance, and tenderness when we touch each other. All good things in marriage.

Let's look specifically at *how* to touch your mate. These are general tips, so see what works for your husband.

Teasing. Typically, you want to use the tips of your fingers or fingernails and work slowly across his skin. Go back and forth, work in circles, or trace your name or a message. Start with less erotic areas and work toward the Big Kahuna.

Here's an interesting trick: Run your fingers along his skin at the edge of his clothing. It doesn't matter whether it's his shirt sleeve or the edge of his underwear, there's something about teasing along that border that is all kinds of sexy.

Stroking. Your hubby should feel your hand substantially touching him. Use your fingers for a lighter touch or your whole hand for more intensity.

Where should you stroke? Anywhere he wants. But try these sensitive male areas: his neck, scalp, ears, lower abdomen, inner thighs. He probably has greater sensitivity anywhere that hair isn't—including backs of knees and inside elbows—but those spots depend on your hubby. Of course, if you want a supercharged reaction, move up from that inner thigh to his penis and get to stroking there.

Massaging. Raise your hand if a back rub has ever turned into a lovemaking session you didn't plan. Yeah, us too. But if you add massage to the plan, you'll likely enjoy the results.

Work with just your hands or add lotion or massage oil for easier movement. Make sure the pressure feels good to your man. Usually guys prefer greater pressure, but not always. (I usually beg my husband to massage my poor muscles harder, while he prefers a lighter touch.) You can rub with your thumbs, fingers, the heels of your hands, palms, or knuckles, but engage your entire hands in one way or another during the massage.

To keep it sensual, start with hubby on his stomach. Progress something like this: neck and shoulders > back and arms > length of his spine > calves > feet > back to thighs > buttocks. Then flip that relaxed man over and get creative.

Grabbing. Most wives don't want to be cooking and suddenly feel their husband's hand squeezing a butt cheek. But men tend to desire more intensity in their wives' touch. Your hubby may think it's super-hot for you to walk up, plant your hand over that rarely used undies flap, and give his little guy a pump or two. That's a cue that can't easily be missed, and he might appreciate a clear signal that you're good-to-go.

During sex, increasing your grip to the level of grabbiness (is that word?) can let your mate know you're edging up the excitement meter. You can grab his shoulders, wrap your hands around the back of his head, or sink your hands into the fleshy cheeks of his backside and give a good squeeze. Or maneuver him into positions that feel particularly good, like grabbing his buttocks to pull him deeper into you.

Touching yourself. Most husbands enjoy watching their wives touch themselves. Why? It's a visual thing. Plus, they get up-close-and-personal tutoring on what turns you on so they can mimic those motions later and get you all hot and bothered with their own hands.

If you've never done this before, it's going to feel weird the first time. And probably the second. Let's face it: Your hand and his hand do not feel the same. Also, having an audience, even if it's only your husband, can make it hard to relax and become aroused.

Be willing to start slow—teasing and stroking yourself like discussed above—and then move to your breasts and vulva. You may want to add lubrication down below.

After that, tune in to what your body wants—be it slow and soft touches or faster movement and increased pressure. If you want to achieve orgasm as he watches, find that knobby bit of flesh above your vagina (your clitoris) and stroke it gently, moving in various ways to see what feels good. Increase speed and pressure as you heat up. For tips on reaching orgasm, check out the chapter on that topic.

Adding touch to intercourse. Your hands can boost stimulation during intercourse. As your husband thrusts, stroke the lower part of his penis, tenderly caress his testicles, or rub your clitoris or breasts. Any of these may add to the arousal you two experience.

This is by no means a comprehensive rundown on what you can do with your hands. Use your imagination to expand on the ideas here. Just keep your hands involved in the sexual encounter.

By the way, in my research, I did find one biblical passage specifically about hands and sex. It comes from—no surprise—Song of Songs: "My beloved thrust his hand through the latch-opening; my heart began to pound for him. I arose to open for my beloved, and my hands dripped with myrrh, my fingers with flowing myrrh, on the handles of the bolt" (5:4–5). Their hands aren't even touching each other yet, simply anticipating when they will. Which can also be arousing.

Let's close this section on using your hands in marital intimacy with one more Bible verse. Ecclesiastes 9:10 says, "Whatever your hand finds to do, do it with all your might." Can I get an amen?

What to Do with Your Mouth

As I did with hands, I looked up all the Bible passages I could find that included the words *mouth*, *lips*, *tongue*, and *kiss*. (Yes, I have a very interesting search history.) Then I did some other research, some of it hands-on (because that's how dedicated I am to helping you).

Following are tips for how to use your mouth in marital lovemaking.

Speak lovingly. The vast majority of Scripture passages with *mouth*, *lips*, or *tongue* relate to what we say. The Bible emphasizes again and again the importance of measuring our words and using them responsibly. I can't be the only one who learned this verse while watching VeggieTales's *Larry Boy and the Rumor Weed*: "Reckless words pierce like a sword, but the tongue of the wise brings healing" (Proverbs 12:18, NIV 1984 ed.).[17] Thanks, Larry Boy! That's a great summary scripture. Words matter.

The lovers in Song of Songs totally got this. To get some examples, read a few chapters and see how the spouses speak of and to each other. The words you speak during lovemaking can tear down your husband or make him feel desired, loved, and adept as a lover. Consider how your mouth can be used to speak words that build up your hubby and your marital intimacy. Then speak 'em!

Pucker up. The first sentence in the Song of Songs is this: "Let him kiss me with the kisses of his mouth—for your love is more delightful than wine." That's a perfect way to start your sexual encounter, using that mouth for some delicious kissing.

You can join lips to lips, mouth to mouth, and tongue to tongue, but you can also kiss almost anywhere on his body. Of course, I am not planning to ever kiss my husband's armpit, but I'd say that almost all of your man's body would love to feel the touch of your lips. And some places may respond particularly well to the soft, wet touch of a kiss. Try a few of these:

His eyelids. Yep, eyelids. They're surprisingly sensitive, and kissing his eyelids means he must close his eyes, which can heighten the sense of touch.

His ears. Kiss those lobes, up the curve of his ear, and behind his ear. Some guys go a little crazy with such kisses.

His neck and collarbone. Nuzzle right in there under his chin and get busy. Move your lips up, down, and all around … and work your way down to his collarbone, which is also sensitive for most men.

His nipples. You're not the only one with sensitive nipples. Maybe his aren't quite so much, but he might still enjoy your mouth hanging out there a bit.

His stomach. Tease your kisses all over his tummy, giving some extra attention around his navel.

His thighs. Maybe it's the proximity to where he'd really like your mouth to be, but your hubby's thighs are likely an erogenous zone. Especially the inner thigh. Move your mouth around in gentle kisses and see if he likes it. (If I were a betting woman, I'd put down a fiver he will.)

His butt. The buttocks are the flipside of his Happytown, and it wouldn't mind your mouth going up and down its hills.

His penis. The mayor of Happytown would definitely love a visit from your lips. His testicles are also sensitive to your touch. But be extra gentle there!

His hands. You didn't expect me to go from the penis to something so seemingly ho-hum as his hands. But our hands are very sensitive, and you can turn him on by kissing his hands, especially the inside of his palm.

Lick it up. Your tongue is a lovely tool for arousal. You can lick any of the places mentioned above.

Be gentle with your tongue in most of these spots. You can use the tip of your tongue to tease and titillate. Think how you might lick an envelope. To give a more intense experience, flatten out your tongue and go at your husband like he's a dripping ice cream scoop. Go slow to draw out the sensation. You can also flick your tongue, moving the tip up and down or side to side.

Nibble. One of the Oxford Dictionary's definitions for *nibble* is to "gently bite at (a part of the body), esp. amorously or nervously." Let's go with amorously.

I didn't look up *teeth* in the Bible, but they're in your mouth and they're awfully handy for providing a stronger touch and a little tug on your husband's flesh. How hard you bite is up to him. Pay attention to his reaction. Some husbands would welcome a little chomp-down on the shoulder or a strong tug on the earlobe. Other hubbies are more sensitive and would rather you focus on the word *gently* in that definition of nibble.

Just don't bite his manly stuff! You do want your husband to survive another day, right?

Suck, the good way. When my husband annoys me and I want to jokingly let him know, my typical statement is "You suck ... and not in the good way." Which gets both of us laughing and defuses any tension that might have been there. But I'm hitting at something true here: sucking is a nice piece of your mouth's lovemaking repertoire.

Don't go all "vacuum" on him; you're not Hoover. But put your mouth on him and pull your lips together in a nice, long, gentle suck. Most places listed above are fair game, but a few spots are also suck-worthy. When you kiss his mouth, you can suck on his lips a little. You could also take each of his fingers and pull them into your mouth for a little sucking. And for a big reaction, suck on the top part of his penis, paying special attention with your tongue to the stretch of flesh that connects the shaft with the head on the lower side (the frenulum).

Once your mouth has given pleasure to your husband, let's hope his response is like the lover in Song of Songs: "Your lips drop sweetness as the honeycomb, my bride; milk and honey are under your tongue" (4:11).

Use these tips to do something you haven't done yet or to revisit something you haven't done in a while. Just think about the wonder of God's gift of your mouth in providing pleasure to your spouse. There are so many ways you can use it.

What to Do with Your Legs

In Song of Songs 7:1, the husband comments on his wife's lovely gams. "Your graceful legs are like jewels, the work of an artist's hands."

Beyond being a beautiful part of the body for him to gaze upon, what can you do with your legs during lovemaking with your husband? For ease, I am defining "legs" here as everything from below your hip down, including your feet.

Touch. You can start by stroking your husband with your legs and/or feet. When you embrace, rub your legs against his legs or torso. Stroke his back or buttocks with your calves or feet. Wrap your legs around his body. Skin-to-skin contact heightens arousal. The more your bodies touch, the better. So involve your legs and feet in touching your man.

You can also use your feet to rub his testicles or his penis. Be gentle! It's a bit harder to control the pressure of your touch with feet than hands, so you'll need to be careful to touch the jewels delicately. But playing "footsie" with his privates could be a big turn-on for your hubby.

Proximity. Your legs are a great way to signal to your husband how close you want him to be. Assuming you're making love face-to-face, you can wrap your legs around his body and pull him in closer with your legs. This is especially useful when he's thrusting and you want him to go deeper.

Of course, your legs can also push him away. For instance, if you want a break to change position, you can use your feet or legs to push him back and reposition your body.

Sexual positioning. Your legs can play a starring role in sexual positioning with your husband. Besides the usual on-the-bed placement, or wrapped around your honey, what can you do with your legs to try different positions?

Legs wide. This may seem obvious, but there are times when you should spread particularly wide. For example, to give your husband a clear view of your private beauty, to provide easy access for oral sex, or to experience a different sensation during intercourse.

Legs together. Closing your legs tighter can provide more pressure on the hubby and provide an interesting sensation for you. This can be done from a front-to-front position, with him behind, spooning, or in several other positions. The closeness of your thighs to knees is what matters.

Legs raised. Positioning your legs and feet up either behind your husband or on him can affect how sexual intercourse feels. Changing your legs' position changes the angle at which your genitals connect, meaning the sensations you experience can change. You may find a position you like particularly well.

What do I mean by "raised"? Options include placing your legs over his shoulders, keeping your legs up and straight, bending your legs and placing your feet on his chest. You can also do these positions while sitting in a chair or, for the adventurous, standing.

Changing up your legs' position can provide different visuals, access, and sensations for you both. Experiment and see how it feels.

Rhythm. Your legs, knees, and feet can also control or contribute to the rhythm of your lovemaking. For instance, by squatting over your husband's body, you can take control of the thrusting yourself, using up-and-down and rocking motions. In a hands-and-knees position, with your husband entering the vagina from behind, you can rock your body on your legs and meet the rhythm he provides. You can also put your feet on his chest, against the wall behind your husband, or on the floor if you're sitting to get some traction for using your legs and pulsing your body against his.

If you've left the thrusting entirely to your husband thus far, I suspect he'd love to see you get involved. Use those legs and move against him in a way that shows you're a happy participant. You might also like taking charge at times, so you can adjust to what feels good to you and increase your pleasure. Which will likely increase his pleasure, since the vast majority of husbands are very aroused seeing their wives aroused.

What to Do with Your Hips

If you look up *hip* in your Bible, you won't find much in the way of romance. There is one mention of how the behemoth's strength is in his hips (Job 40:16 NKJV), but if a husband dared to bring that reference into the bedroom, he'd deserve the glacier-melting glare he got from his wife.

In the two passages in Song of Songs where the husband describes the beauty of his wife's body (chapters 4 and 7), he skips right over the pelvic area. Legs are described. Waist is described. But not what comes in between, even though it's a rather important part of the whole deal. Instead, the lover (husband) primarily refers to his wife's lady parts with symbolic language, such as "garden."

Yet the way God designed a woman's hips allows them to be somewhat of a wonder worker in sexual intimacy with her husband. If she knows how to use them.

Using your hips in marital intimacy mainly entails the motions you can make with them.

Tilting. Front-to-back, your hips work like a pendulum. Tilting them toward your husband can alter the angle of entry and the resulting sensations you both feel. It can also signal to him that you are fully engaged in what's happening.

When making love face-to-face, you can tilt your hips forward, which may allow your husband to move in deeper. In the rear-entry position, tilting your hips backward opens up the area for him to engage more fully.

Rocking. With that same pendulum motion, you can rock your hips forward and backward. This is one of the ways a wife can take control of some of the thrusting. It is easiest done with the woman-on-top position, where she can pulse her hips in a consistent rhythm.

Altering the speed of rocking can affect whether this is a playful motion that draws out lovemaking or a more intense motion that draws toward climax. Advantages of this position and motion are that the husband has a wonderful view of his wife's body, and he can continue to touch her breasts and clitoris to increase her pleasure.

Wiggling. Wiggling is like fidgeting your hips around in a chair, but you're moving around on your husband instead. This tease with your hips can be very enjoyable to both of you as you pay attention to the way your body parts connect and alter slightly with each movement. Be careful not to wiggle too much or too fast, since his erect penis is not meant to be that flexible.

Riding. If you've ever been on a horse (or an elephant or a camel), you know that feeling of your hips bouncing up and down as the animal trots or gallops. That same up-and-down bouncing motion can be incredibly hot during sex.

The wife moves her hips straight up and down, creating the rhythmic thrust for making love. She does the work, but she's also more in control of her pleasure. If needed, she can slow down the pace to draw out her arousal, perhaps increasing the likelihood that she will achieve climax along with her husband during intercourse. Her husband can signal what he desires by placing his hands outside her hips and guiding her.

The best way to "ride" is to plant your feet (the way an equestrian uses stirrups), then squat over your husband. This allows more control than kneeling. Your knees and hips can act together to provide that up-and-down motion. If your legs tire, change to kneeling for a bit and then return to squatting. Or let your husband flip you over and take charge (which he'll probably be happy to do, because he's likely very turned on by how active you are in this sexual encounter).

Heart and Soul

While I believe marriages can benefit from specific coaching and tips (or I wouldn't have bothered to write this book), I don't believe technique is as important as other factors. It's quite possible for both participants to be technically fabulous lovers and not experience fulfilling sexual intimacy.

How do I know? Because, sadly, I've had both experiences. What is the biggest difference between my premarital sexual encounters and my marital sexual encounters? The former attempted to have meaning (and failed), but the latter has deep, deep meaning.

Why? Because my marital intimacy is born of an entirely different relationship: one that involves committed, covenant love … years of shared sorrows, joys, tears, and laughter … security and hope for the future … and the blessing of our heavenly Father. For sexual intimacy to be the full gift God intends it to be, it must involve the heart and soul of both husband and wife.

Song of Songs describes the beautiful sexual love between a husband and a wife. The passages are romantic, passionate, and—if you read 'em right—can be titillating. In the last chapter of this book of Scripture, we get a clear picture of what makes their sexual love so meaningful. The wife declares:

> Place me like a seal over your heart,
> like a seal on your arm;
> for love is as strong as death,
> its jealousy unyielding as the grave.
> It burns like blazing fire,

like a mighty flame.
Many waters cannot quench love;
rivers cannot sweep it away.
If one were to give
all the wealth of one's house for love,
it would be utterly scorned.

Song of Songs 8:6–7

"Like a seal over your heart." The best sexual love involves the heart. Not the momentary rush of emotions in the heart, but a deeper commitment of the heart—like a seal.

A seal in Bible times was used to "guarantee security or indicate ownership"[18]—the kind of I'm-yours-you're-mine commitment that exists in a godly marriage. Indeed, the wife in Song of Songs says that very thing: "My beloved is mine and I am his" (2:16; see also 6:3).

It's like the phrase "heart and soul," which means completely, wholly, totally. In a sense, your sexual encounters should remind you of your wedding vows when you said to your mate, "This is it. I am *all in*."

Sometimes we wives hold back on that emotional and spiritual connection with our husbands. Too many women feel sex is merely a physical act—a pleasurable physiological experience or a release of body tension. God intended it to mean so much more:

> "Haven't you read," he replied, "that at the beginning the Creator 'made them male and female,' and said, 'For this reason a man will leave his father and mother and be united to his wife, and the two will become one flesh'? So they are no longer two, but one flesh. Therefore what God has joined together, let no one separate." (Matthew 19:4–6)

Look for ways to engage your heart and soul in lovemaking with your husband. Be tender, be active, be intimate. Express your love both verbally and physically in the bedroom. Remind yourself that sexuality is a gift for marriage from our Lord and Father—that it came from His heart to bless ours.

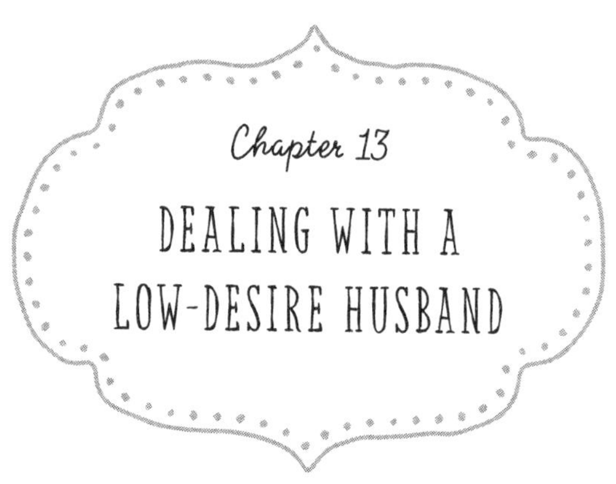

Chapter 13
DEALING WITH A LOW-DESIRE HUSBAND

Do you desire sex more frequently and more intensely than your husband does? That doesn't make you weird. And yet, sometimes, higher-drive wives feel like Vaquita porpoises. (They're among the most endangered species.)

But forget the porpoise, and let's talk purpose. What's your mission as a higher-drive wife?

> All night long on my bed
> I looked for the one my heart loves;
> I looked for him but did not find him.
>
> Song of Songs 3:1

Questions Higher-Desire Wives Ask

Men are always hot for sex, while women are lukewarm to cold much of the time. That's what society, and many churches now, tell us. So it must be true, right?

Not always.

Some wives wonder what's wrong with them or their marriage because they desire a physically intimate relationship but their hubbies don't. It's the hush-hush secret we don't discuss, and as a result, these wives are silently suffering.

What happens when a woman wants sex and her husband doesn't? Most women start to ask themselves one or more of the following questions:

What's wrong with me? *If all husbands are panting and grabbing after their women 24/7 and mine barely glances my direction when I don a sheer negligee, is there something about me that is distasteful? Am I unattractive? Why doesn't he find me physically pleasing?*

There's almost certainly nothing wrong with you. Some couples with amazing sex lives would never get a call from a modeling agency or were poster people for the geek club in high school. It's a fallacy to think that rock stars and Victoria's Secret models are the ones with high sex drives and satisfaction. Most wives don't need to look like Jessica Rabbit to get their hubbies hopping.

Your husband desired you enough to marry you. As long as you're keeping yourself up reasonably well, he should still find you attractive. If he doesn't, there is something amiss with his standards. There are things you can do that might turn your hubby's head, but a man who has almost no sex drive is probably not going to respond merely because you throw on a black lace teddy.

Is he having an affair? *If men think about sex every seven seconds and my hubby hasn't thought about it in three weeks, is he getting his fix elsewhere? Is he not pursuing me because he's already caught another woman?*

Some men do have affairs. But if you have no other clues in that direction, this is probably not the case. Moreover, married men in affairs may continue to have sex with their wives, so lack of interest isn't overwhelming evidence of infidelity. It's probably just evidence of lack of interest.

Is he gay? *Is he simply not interested in sex with women generally? Is he desirous of another kind of relationship? Could he possibly be homosexual?*

There are no good statistics on how many spouses eventually "come out" as homosexual, but it isn't common. If you have no other hints that your husband could be gay, he most likely isn't. Lack of sex drive is not a good clue for sexual orientation.

Is our marriage over? *Does he not find me physically attractive because he is simply no longer in love with me? Does he not want a sexual relationship because he doesn't want any kind of relationship with me?*

If you have a good relationship otherwise, you can most likely improve the sexual area of your marital life as well. If you are not experiencing a good marital relationship overall and your sex life is also poor, you should seek professional help. If your husband will not go with you, go alone and see if the counselor has suggestions for what you can do to positively impact you both.

Is something physically wrong with him? *Is the problem with his body just not responding?* This is the most likely reason for your husband's lack of interest. A sufficient amount of testosterone is required for a man to experience a normal sex drive. If he is low on this hormone, his sex drive will decrease. Low thyroid levels, depression, high blood sugar, and other factors can also affect a man's libido. In addition, negative events from the past can impede a husband's desire and enjoyment of sex with his wife. If your husband was molested or inappropriately exposed to sexual material as a child, that could be suppressing his ability to engage in appropriate physical intimacy now. Porn use has also been implicated in the lowering of men's sex drives by causing physiological changes in the brain's mode of arousal.[19]

What can I do to improve our sex life? *If I bring up this subject, will I embarrass him? Will he be angry? Hurt? Even less attracted to me? Is there any fix available?*

You must bring up the topic if you want to see any improvement. If you are concerned that he will be embarrassed, angry, or hurt, schedule a therapy session with a Christian marriage counselor and address it in that safe environment. If you can talk to him alone, schedule a time away from the children and other interruptions, and find a place with privacy and quiet.

Once you're able to sit and talk, do not complain about the lack of sex or unleash your theories about why he doesn't desire you. Rather, explain that you are concerned about your physical relationship, that you desire greater physical intimacy, and that you want to address any issues affecting your lack of connection in that area. If there was a time when things were better, you can reference a "remember when ..." and explain that you want to experience that closeness again.

Is this as good as it gets? *Am I relegated to a sexless marriage? If it never gets any better, how can I remain in this marriage?*

A sexless marriage is *not* what God intended. Having said that, if my husband was physically injured tomorrow in a way that made it impossible for us to be physically intimate, would I stay with him? Absolutely! Still, I understand that being unable to perform and being unwilling to engage are two different things.

Spend time in prayer asking for God's help to work through the hurt and the loneliness you feel. Sex is not the only reason to be married; there are many benefits to having a relationship with your husband.

Women whose husbands have sexually neglected them tend to go through a self-evaluation more extensive than the battery of tests given to a patient on psychiatric commitment. It's okay to ponder the problem, but not good to obsess and question every little thing about yourself or your marriage. Address the issue, seek help if needed, and pray for greater physical intimacy.

Internal Factors

How can you biblically and practically approach your husband's low sexual desire? Let's start with this: You cannot change your spouse. You cannot make your husband have sex with you. The transformation must come from him.

There are, however, internal and external factors that influence our decisions. For instance, I eat when I feel hungry (internal) and when someone puts a brownie in front of my face (external). I won't eat unless I make a decision to, but things happening in and around me impact my choices.

Internal factors are what's going on inside your husband and may include:

issues (past or present) with pornography that distort his perception of sexuality
low testosterone
depression
a history of sexual abuse
stress from job or other responsibilities
guilt from prior promiscuity
a lack of self-confidence

Just as you can't control your husband's hunger, you can't control factors impacting his low sexual drive. Yet you can help him identify what's happening. Unfortunately, we wives often choose the worst ways to get our husbands to recognize a problem. Do any of these sound familiar?

nagging
pleading
demanding
shoving information and research in his face
sharing the story of your cousin or your friend's husband

over-the-top crying
quoting Scripture at him
threatening
giving ultimatums
saying "If you loved me, you'd ..."

These tactics make conversation unpleasant and tense, and many husbands will run from that faster than Road Runner from Wile E. Coyote.

Yes, 1 Corinthians 7:4–5 says, "The wife does not have authority over her own body but yields it to her husband. In the same way, the husband does not have authority over his own body but yields it to his wife. Do not deprive each other except perhaps by mutual consent and for a time, so that you may devote yourselves to prayer." That verse indicates it's a sin to deprive your spouse. The Bible commands us not to. But how can you point out that sin to your husband?

Consider Matthew 7:12: "In everything, do to others what you would have them do to you." If a husband is struggling with depression, a pornography addiction, or past abuse, he doesn't want to be slammed on the head with what else is wrong with him. But he does need to deal with those issues. Ask yourself how you can create a safe environment for the two of you to openly discuss marital intimacy.

Find a good place and time to talk. The worst place is in the bedroom and the worst time is after you've offered sex and he's declined. Choose a time when you are not sexually charged or feeling particularly hurt. You may even need to get away from the house, although make sure you're in a private setting. Keep your clothes on. Men often talk more easily shoulder-to-shoulder than face-to-face, so try a fishing trip, golfing, a nature hike, touring a sculpture garden—whatever suits your fancy and his.

Don't make statements. Ask questions.

How do you think our marriage is going overall?

Growing up, who were your role models for marriage? How do you think they influenced you?

What do you wish you had done differently before marriage regarding sexuality? What are you glad you did right?

Before we married, what did you think our sex life would be like?

What would you like our sex life to be like?

How frequently would you like to make love?

What turns you on? What turns you off?

How can I be a better lover to you?

Now, don't grill the poor guy. This isn't the Spanish Inquisition where you expect him to recant his heresy and adopt your doctrine on the spot. Choose a question or two at a time and let the conversation unfold. It may take several outings and weeks or even months to get to the heart of the problems. But you aren't simply gathering information. You're demonstrating by your attitude and approach that you're a trustworthy confidante regarding this topic and want the best for both of you.

Adopt a "we" attitude. Whatever his issue is, it is yours to tackle *together*. You're married—one flesh. And consider this: he could return that favor if someday you struggle with hormonal issues or depression that affects your libido. Assure him that whatever the issue is, you aren't there to wave it around in front of him. You want to be the helper that God described in Genesis 2:18.

Express your desire for intimacy, not just frequency. No one likes to be used. Which is one of the reasons a lower-drive spouse can react like a prodded cobra when the higher-drive spouse says she wants more sex. He may not feel loved so much as used to meet a physical need.

Of course, you and I know that's not the reality. If you only wanted to release sexual tension, you could get that done without engaging your husband. Sex, however, is a physical expression of affection and also fosters closeness between you. Focus your discussion on how you desire to engage with your husband in intimacy because you want that closeness.

Go for a win-win. Ask your husband to help you find a solution that's not merely a compromise but that meets both parties' needs and desires. You may require a mediator to find that win-win. Perhaps your hubby will agree to meet a few times with a counselor or your pastor and brainstorm ways for both of you to get what you want out of your intimacy.

Pray. Cover every step with prayer. And don't make it "Dear God, please change my husband from being a selfish, ignorant jerk to a sweet, passionate lover." Pray for your husband to have the delight of sex with you. Pray for you to delight in him. Pray for you to reach accord.

When words fail you, and even when they don't, pray the Scriptures. Proverbs 5:18–19 is a great verse to pray. Here's my translation: "Dear God, I pray that my husband's fountain will be blessed, that he will find reasons to rejoice in me and our marriage. I pray he will see me as loving and graceful and that my breasts will always satisfy him. I pray he will become intoxicated by my love." Can I get an amen for that?

Remember, you can't change your husband. The only person you can control is *you*! So take a deep breath, commit to being the best wife you can be, and do what you can to create a more intimate marriage.

External Factors

Why don't you hear more about high-drive wives? Here are some of the reasons people tend not to talk about the wife being the higher-desire spouse.

(1) What husband wants to admit he isn't the stereotypical sex-craving man?

(2) Wives who express their desire for more sex are often shut down by other wives with statements like "I wish my husband would lay off" or even "You're lucky."

(3) We tend to discuss all topics from the point of view of the "typical." Don't believe me? Read a parenting book. If my child was the "average," he would have slept through the night within weeks of his birth, stayed in time-out after three tries, and been potty-trained at age two. Yeah, that didn't happen. Likewise, no spouse or marriage is "average" in every way.

Earlier we looked at internal factors that might affect your husband's lack of interest and tips for bringing up the subject without starting a wildfire in your home. However, some wives report their husbands won't listen, no matter what. What then?

Here's my advice: Stop talking about it. I'm not suggesting you stop addressing it. Just stop addressing it with *words*. If this is a volatile subject in your house, you both need time to defuse. Lay off for a while, maybe three to six months. In the meantime, communicate without words.

Communicate your desirability in other ways, which might influence him externally to take a greater interest in sexual intimacy. Be the kind of wife who draws a husband closer.

Now, I'm not talking about donning a lace teddy and stilettos, calling him "Big Boy," and offering to live out some sexual fantasy. While I'm not opposed to such things, they're the toppings, not the cake. You might get a guy to have sex with you by looking like a *Cosmo* cover, but that's not marital intimacy. Ultimately, you want a sex life with substance and intimacy, so you have to invest in the relationship cake before you add a little icing.

Besides, you'll only feel worse if you decorate your bedroom like a love den, put on candles and music, show up in your sexiest get-up, and he ignores or outright refuses you. You don't want to end that night with him snoring and you dripping tears into your pillow as you wonder, again, what's wrong with you.

So, how can you be a more desirable wife to your husband?

Invest in the friendship. Sheila Gregoire, in her book *The Good Girl's Guide to Great Sex*, says that if you want your husband to desire you sexually, first you need to be someone he wants to be around generally.[20] When the relationship is stressful, it's harder for most people to engage willingly and become vulnerable in the bedroom.

Although it doesn't all rest with you, do everything in your power to be an appealing person. Are you a nagging wife? Do you disrespect your husband with your words or your body language? Is your home always a place of tension or mayhem? What issues might you need to address?

Have you forgotten how to play and laugh with each other? Do you make time for a weekly date night—even if it's hot cocoa and conversation on the couch after the kids have gone to bed? Do you ask about his job, his interests, his friendships, and then listen and support his answers? Do you find activities you both enjoy doing together?

Your husband may be more willing to discuss deep issues and/or engage with you physically if he feels accepted and valued emotionally in the relationship. Make sure you haven't neglected this area. You want him to be your friend, right? Be his friend too.

Focus on affection. While friendship is an important aspect of marriage, sexless marriages often look like roommate arrangements. I don't know about you, but I have friends who would make easier roommates than my husband. Some of my girlfriends can cook like a Food Network show host, would aim at my toilet successfully every time, and would happily watch chick flicks with me. And I'd never have to clean facial hair out of the sink again. But I didn't get married simply for a roommate. I want the other goodies too.

Even if you aren't getting the main event from your husband, you can enjoy more with him than you would with a roomie. I don't snuggle with my BFF, but I do with my husband. Physical affection is a precursor to more intimate physical activity. Hold hands, kiss, hug, stroke him lovingly. All without expectation of it leading to the bedroom.

The paradox is that ongoing physical affection without the expectation of sexual reward can lead to sexual reward. Moreover, an embrace lasting longer than twenty seconds can cause a release of oxytocin—the body's bonding chemical, which is also released by men at sexual climax. So affection may awaken the physical arousal side of your husband, and it introduces loving touch in a low-pressure context.

Engage in skin-to-skin contact. There is something about having your skin brush up against your husband's that can tap into inner arousal. Go to bed wearing as little as possible without being obvious you want sex. For instance, keep the lace teddy in the drawer, but wear a cotton cami and undies to bed. Play footsie under the table at breakfast. Offer to put lotion or oil on his tired muscles or give him a massage. Ask for lotion or a massage from him. Whatever gets you touching each other may help to reawaken his natural desire for physical intimacy.

Change your timing. Some people struggle with feeling stressed or tired by nightfall and having enough energy for love-making. Try initiating sex in the morning. A man's testosterone levels are highest at that time of day, and men typically awaken with a "maintenance erection." I know a couple who has sex every Saturday morning because that happens to be the best time for them to engage. My hubby and I have found that afternoon or early evening is usually best for us. If nighttime has been your usual window for sex, see if you have better results at a different time of day.

Your sex life doesn't all depend upon you; your husband must make the decision to engage. But I've heard from married couples who had poor sex lives for years, experienced a turnaround, and are now livin' it up in the bedroom. Those couples are glad they didn't give up.

Are there guarantees? No. Is there hope? Absolutely. God desires that you both have a healthy, fulfilling intimacy, and He can redeem any situation.

Be assured that change can happen. Every single day, marriages improve. Spouses break through obstacles, connect where they were divided, reignite the spark.

And when you feel doubt, you can always find confidence in the Lord.

I cried out, "I am slipping!"
but your unfailing love, O Lord, supported me.
When doubts filled my mind,
your comfort gave me renewed hope and cheer.

Psalm 94:18–19 (NLT)

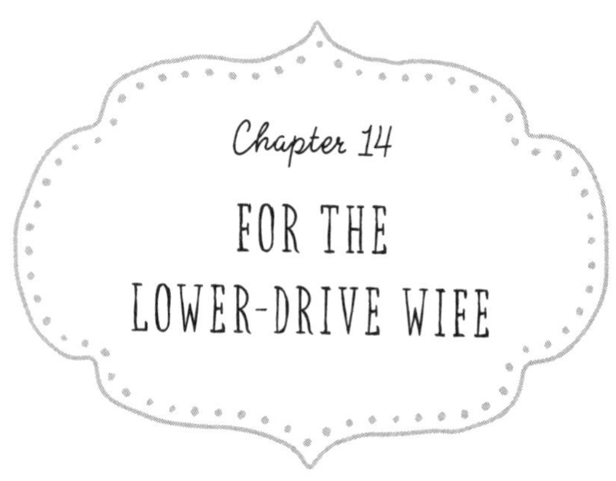

Chapter 14
FOR THE LOWER-DRIVE WIFE

All this talk of sex, and you're not even that interested … if at all. What do you do when you're the lower-desire spouse? Must you engage in all this sex to have a good marriage?

Sex is indeed one of God's provisions for marriage, but He doesn't want you to do it with a sense of duty and dread. He wants to bless you with intimacy and pleasure. It's time to "awaken love" and see the marriage bed in a different light.

How handsome you are, my beloved!
Oh, how charming!
And our bed is verdant.
Song of Songs 1:16

When You Don't Desire Sex

Your sex drive is low or nonexistent. You understand the importance of sex in your marriage, but you really could take or leave it. How can you turn that libido switch on?

Let's talk about some potential causes for your low libido.

Your physiology is messed up. God designed us to be sexual beings who desire intimate contact with our spouses. While we may differ in our desire for frequency, having no desire at all indicates something else is going on. The first thing to do is to check with your doctor.

Get an appointment with your primary care physician or gynecologist and explain your lack of libido. Get tested for hormone levels and vitamin deficiencies. Make sure you are not suffering from major depression, which can cause a drop in libido. (Ironically, some antidepressants can also cause a drop in libido.) Are you on birth control? Research has recently reported a link between oral contraception and lack of desire.[21]

You have negative sexual occurrences in your past. Anything in your past that causes you to consider sex a negative activity can impact how you approach your husband and marital intimacy now. Were you sexually abused as a child? Were you harassed? Did you blossom early and receive taunting? Were you raped? Were you told sex was dirty? Did you engage in promiscuous behavior that left you with guilt? Was your first time a disappointment or painful? Have you struggled with pornography?

Let me indulge in another food analogy. Even if you know your grandmother thoroughly washed and cooked the shrimp she's serving, if you got food poisoning the last time you ate shrimp, you will not be eager to pop a shellfish into your mouth. The physiological and emotional responses of that prior negative experience are imprinted on you. In the same way, anything sexual in your past that left you with a bad taste in your mouth can make you reluctant to take another bite.

Deal with your past. Acknowledge what happened and how you were affected. Work through how it hurt you and how you can change the way you view that time. Psychologists often suggest writing a letter to someone involved, or even to yourself, to air out your full feelings and get perspective. (But don't send it.) See a quality Christian counselor if you need to. Then rewrite the script.

The best way to see marital intimacy as a positive thing is to have positive marital experiences. Make your intimacy so much better than the negative past that your brain and heart change direction and see how sex really is a blessing from God in the right context.

You're not in touch with your body. To enjoy sex, you need to be able to relax and remain aware of the sensations of your body. If you have difficulty letting go, you may not be sensitive enough to arousal to enjoy the experience. Train yourself to notice how your body feels with different touches and textures. Try a set of satin sheets. Take bubble baths and notice the way the water feels on your skin. Invite your husband to apply lotion or oil to your body. Learn to focus and be more cognizant of how your body is feeling in various ways. That will make you more open to arousal during physical intimacy.

You're not great lovers. When a wife tells me she has hated sex for twenty years, I sometimes wonder, *What's her husband doing wrong?* Technique is not the be-all and end-all of sexuality. However, if your mate doesn't know how to turn you on, or you don't know how to help yourself get there, the sex may not feel very good.

Some couples have wonderful relationships, great attitudes, and a desire to connect, but what they need is a little skills training. Before you hire a coach to come into your bedroom—*God forbid*—let me say that you can learn all you need to know from books, blogs, communication, trial-and-error, and trial-and-success. More important, you can communicate with your mate.

Take time to explore each other and let him know how you become aroused.

You have a poor self-image. God has made women beautiful, and we have a desire to be and feel beautiful. Yet we ladies have way too much pressure to look a certain way. If you dislike your own body, it's not easy to share that body with your husband. You don't want to be naked, you don't want to be touched, you tense up when your body is exposed.

However, beauty comes in all shapes and sizes. Having heard from many men on this subject, let me assure you that you are beautiful to your hubby. Even if magazine models seem to put you to shame (and even those beautiful models are airbrushed, so they don't look like that either), you can confidently enter your own bedroom and know your husband appreciates the way you look. Believe God's assertion that you are beautiful and believe your husband when he says he desires you.

Your relationship is having difficulties. If your relationship outside the bedroom is in distress, you may not want to make love with your husband. It's been said that men have sex to feel loved, and women have to feel loved to have sex. Wives need a sense of security and value in the marriage to be able to open up in the bedroom.

Address relationship issues as they arise in as noncombative a way as possible. Seek counseling if the issues are big or persistent. Do not withhold sex, however, unless there are severe issues that call for that extreme measure. Continuing to connect physically can help to weather storms in marriage, and husbands in particular are more motivated to work on the relationship if they are happy with their wives in the bedroom.

Stress is sucking the life out of your libido. Stress comes from many places and shows up in various forms. You may be stressed from work demands, household responsibilities, child care, family issues, bouts of illness, etc. It may manifest as sadness, anger, escapism, sleep deprivation, fatigue. Stress is a mood killer all around.

While sex can relieve stress, it can be difficult for women to shift into enjoyment of sex when stress has its grip on them. Husbands are usually better able to let everything else go and focus on the moment, although stress can affect their libido as well. Wives need to be able to relax and surrender to the physical sensations they are having to become aroused and engaged. If stress is overwhelming your day-to-day life, you may not realize it's taking a toll on your sex life too.

What to do about stress? First, prioritize your life. Say no to things you don't need to take on. Eating healthy and exercising are wonderful ways to care for yourself and to relieve stress.

And make sure you have someone to talk to. Don't dump everything on your hubby. Talk about what's bugging you to a best friend, a family member, a counselor, or a mentor so that stress isn't building inside you.

Meditation has also been shown to relieve tension. Find a quiet spot for reflection and follow the psalmist's example: "I meditate on your precepts and consider your ways." (This is 119:15, but the whole chapter is full of references to meditation.)

Finally, pray. Dump your heart on God. The Bible is full of examples of godly people laying all their troubles before Him. And Jesus said, "Come to me, all you who are weary and burdened, and I will give you rest" (Matthew 11:28).

Find the source of your lack of libido, and address it. You and your marriage will benefit.

Two Words Your Higher-Desire Spouse Needs You to Hear

Higher-drive spouses are looking for a secret formula to coax their lower-drive mates into the marriage bed, the perfect approach to get across what they really want, the magic words to launch a new era of satisfying sexual intimacy.

I can break it down to two words: *show up*.

This isn't the whole of the matter, but it is a good starting place. Here's what I mean.

Show up with your presence. Comedian and filmmaker Woody Allen once said, "Showing up is eighty percent of life."[22] He's got a point. You have to show up to your job, show up to buy groceries, show up to study your Bible. You can't accomplish anything in life if you aren't actually there.

God is pretty clear that you're supposed to show up to your marriage bed. "The husband should fulfill his marital duty to his wife, and likewise the wife to her husband" (1 Corinthians 7:3).

You have a "marital duty" to your spouse, the same kind of duty as feeding your children or working your job or going to church. Don't stay away from the marriage bed for too long.

With this admonition, many low-drive spouses imagine being at the beck and call of a sex-addicted spouse. I'm not saying that. Consider that day job again. You can call in sick sometimes, right? But if you call in sick over and over and over, eventually you don't have a job anymore. If you "call in sick" with the marriage bed again and again, eventually you won't have much of a marriage.

You might feel a-okay about things, but for your higher-drive spouse, your continual refusals to be present in the marriage bed feel like refusals to show up to the relationship at all.

Show up with your whole self. One of my sons struggled to understand that sitting in a desk at school wasn't a sufficient amount of showing up to learn anything or earn good grades. (Ah, parenthood!) Sometimes being present isn't really showing up. Sure, you're physically there, but everything about your attitude, your expression, your focus indicates you'd rather be somewhere else.

That's how some spouses treat 1 Corinthians 7. "Hey, I showed up. What more does my man want?" You wouldn't enjoy your husband showing up to a conversation or a date night with a sourpuss attitude and no engagement in the experience. Likewise, it isn't enough to give minimum effort to your sexual intimacy. If your hubby only wanted a physical release, he could do that on his own. He wants *you*—fully present and engaged and enjoying the encounter. Moreover, God intended sex as a gift to both of you.

Decide to be present—heart, body, and soul. Cast off distractions and concentrate on physical sensations and close body contact. Prioritize this moment and give yourself fully to it. Show up with your whole self. You might be surprised how much more you'll enjoy sex.

Show up on your own. No one likes having to drag their loved one to an event or activity. Some spouses do it (have you seen that poor guy slumped in a chair outside the department store dressing room?), but it's not enjoyable for anyone. It's much more loving to offer to accompany your honey when you know an event is important to him. Got a hubby who likes to fish? Offer to go out on the boat with him. Does he like to dance? Offer to take lessons together. Your higher-desire husband wants to have sex? Initiate.

Maybe you don't have an independent desire for sexual intimacy. That's okay. Remember when those physical sensations and the embracing of your bodies felt really good, and let that inspire you. Or imagine how pleasurable it could be if you spoke up about something you'd like to try in the bedroom. Then prepare yourself as best you can for your sexual event by removing distractions and setting the scene and awakening your senses.

Step outside your comfort zone now and then, and initiate. Your willingness to show up on your own will go a long way toward making your spouse feel loved.

Do You Make Your Husband Feel Guilty about Sex?

A lot of husbands are guilt-ridden. They go week to week, month to month, sexual encounter to sexual encounter, feeling bad about themselves and their marriage.

Why? Because they want sex, even report they need sex, but their wives aren't engaged. What factors evoke these feelings of guilt?

She thinks it's dirty. This wife was taught that sex was something bad girls do, a mere act of the flesh that godly women don't desire or enjoy. Or maybe she experienced sexual misuse or abuse in her past and she can't imagine sex being a truly good thing.

So when her husband craves her body and the ecstasy of lovemaking, he feels bad. He knows she doesn't desire it, doesn't enjoy it, thinks he's a lesser creature for even wanting such a sordid act so often. But he can't get rid of his sex drive. He wants his beloved woman deeply, desperately. What can he do? How can he get past the guilt of constantly wanting to be one flesh with his wife?

She doesn't have time for it. This wife is busy with the demands of being a wife, household manager, mother, worker, and whatever other roles she's balancing. She understands sex is important, but can't her husband see it's secondary to the higher purposes of her life? Perhaps she's running a ministry, something that makes a genuine difference in people's lives, and her husband feels guilty for taking her away from her calling.

He feels selfish for demanding her time and attention, for feeling jealous of others who get her time and attention, for not being able to go without. Yet his body trembles with desire for her, and he simply can't get out of his mind the longing to connect with her physically.

She rejects his advances. Most times he asks, this wife turns him down. He knows she doesn't want sex, not anywhere near like he does, and he can't fully understand. Doesn't she love him? Maybe the problem is with him, that he wants it too much.

Should he simply pray for God to douse his desire, leave him content with those few times she is willing? He hates to ask again, but it's been so long and he wants to have sex—with her. How can he move beyond the rejection?

She doesn't enjoy it. This wife will oblige her husband's advances, but her attitude screams, *This is for you only!* Maybe she believes she's being truly loving, offering her body to him for his satisfaction. And because he wants sex so much, he partakes.

His satisfaction is bittersweet. He feels like he's using her for his own gratification, when what he really desires is for her to enjoy the experience like he does. He feels trapped. His only choices seem to be refusing the sex he wants so much or continuing to feel like a clod for having his way with her.

She downplays her enjoyment. This wife willingly engages, but she discounts her own sexual needs and desires. She doesn't take the extra effort to figure out her body and what feels good.

She won't communicate what she likes, even when asked. She skips the orgasm more often than not, perhaps proclaiming it's not worth it. Her downplaying of enjoyment conveys she doesn't feel like she's worth it.

Her husband yearns to bring her pleasure. He revels in those few times she goes over the top, to the peak of sexual arousal. He feels guilty when he can't bring her there, when she doesn't let him focus on her, when the balance of sex is mostly for him. If only he could help her understand how turned on it makes him to turn her on.

It's easy to misconstrue your man's eager advances as a merely physical desire to "get his jollies." Some men do approach sex like that, especially in single life and secular culture.

However, I also hear from husbands about how much sex means to them. How it's not just about the physical release. Of course, it *is* about the physical release somewhat; that body craving to be intimate with the person you love is a God-given biological desire. But sex means more than that. It's an expression of deep love and connection. Husbands feel loved and confident and whole when they experience regular, mutual sexual satisfaction with their wives.

Sex was God's idea. It is to be enjoyed in the confines of a covenant marriage. It should be mutually sought and satisfying. It is a good thing.

Do you make your husband feel guilty for wanting that?

Think about what messages you intentionally or unintentionally send about the meaning of sex in your relationship. Whatever obstacle prevents you from fully engaging in God's gift of sexual intimacy, address it today. Help your husband receive what God intended him to have—the intimacy he can only receive from you, his chosen beloved.

Three Things Higher-Drive Husbands Long For

You might think the three things higher-drive husbands long for are sex, sex, and sex. But while I'm certain higher-drive husbands would like greater frequency of sexual intimacy in marriage, I truly believe they want more. Here are three other important things higher-drive spouses long for.

Recognition that their sex drive isn't bad. When you want physical intimacy a lot, and your wife doesn't, you can get the feeling your sex drive is a bad thing. Sometimes it's just a feeling that you want sex more than you want to want it. Other times it's expressed by your wife with statements like "Stop being so selfish" or questions like "Why do you want sex all the time?"—usually accompanied by a haughty tone and a sneer.

Rather than embracing your libido, you start to feel less-than, in your eyes and/or your wife's. And that's a horrible thing to feel about something that should be considered a gift from God.

Your hubby wants you to recognize that his sex drive isn't bad. It's not inherently selfish or evil or disgusting. A strong desire to make love with your covenant wife is a beautiful thing.

Understanding that sex isn't just about sex. Sure, some husbands are completely into the physical side of sex and don't understand the deeper implications. But many more higher-drive hubbies want sex not simply for physical satisfaction, but because it makes them feel connected, loved, and intimate with their wives.

A higher-drive husband doesn't see his wife as a mere tool for achieving a goal. No way! Even if words fail him and he seems to default to talking about the sex itself, if you could dig deep and tease out what's really happening, you'd discover that sex is powerfully meaningful to him.

He wants the physical pleasure, but he wants the whole package—physical, recreational, emotional, spiritual. And more than anything, the higher-drive husband wants to feel the love of his wife.

Commitment to try. The mismatch in drives can be frustrating, but what really hurts is a wife unwilling to even try. It pains the heart of a husband longing to show love in the bedroom to be rebuffed and refused constantly, with no hope in sight of anything ever changing. What would help a lot is a simple commitment to try—try to talk about it, try to see another point of view, try to get in the mood, try to change things up a little now and then, try enjoying yourself in bed.

Most higher-drive husbands don't expect an immediate turnaround in their less-willing wives. While it would be great to come home one day and find his beloved with bedroom eyes, little clothing on her body, and rip-raring to go, that's not his expectation or intent. He just wants his wife to love him enough to try to understand and meet his needs—just as they should each be doing in other areas of marriage. The higher-drive hubby isn't looking for a quick change but rather a long-term commitment to invest in sexual intimacy.

Just Because He Stopped Asking, That Doesn't Mean He Stopped Wanting

Husband has a higher drive, and wife has a lesser drive. Husband asks, pursues, begs, pleads, prays, asks, wonders … and finally stops. Wife, meanwhile, feels frustrated, cajoled, annoyed, resentful … and finally relieved.

Wife is glad the constant demands for sex have finally ceased. She figures hubby got the message that having sex once a week—or once a month or less—is more than sufficient for their marriage. Wife believes husband has matured to the point of not acting like a horny teenager or a silly newlywed. Now they are in a calmer stage of their marriage, no longer arguing about when the next sexual encounter will be or why her libido isn't as strong. Surely this is much better—not arguing about sex all the time.

Meanwhile, husband stopped pursuing sex because he was so pained by the personal rejection. Having put himself out there over and over again and done everything he can think of to appeal to his wife and experience the kind of intimacy he desperately desires, he simply can't stand the thought of setting himself up for more refusal.

Has his desire to be physically intimate disappeared? No. It still lingers like a hungry person waiting to be fed. But instead of reaching out with both hands, that hungry sex drive cowers in a corner and waits to be called to the table.

When your husband stops asking, it doesn't mean he has stopped wanting. It means he has given up. And giving up on an important aspect of your relationship is never good for the whole marriage.

Of course we should sacrifice selfishness and petty complaints that don't really matter to the health of our marriage. But wanting to express and grow our affection for each other in physical union isn't selfish or petty. In fact, spouses don't stop asking for sex only to avoid the hurt, but oftentimes to avoid conflict in the marriage. They sacrifice their sexual desire for the sake of peace.

Yet that "peace" is shaky. It's not real.

One of the worst things to see in a couple whose marriage is on the rocks is a spouse who shows no interest in arguing through anything. The spouse's unwillingness to deal with issues likely indicates that he or she has disengaged from the relationship, that this spouse no longer believes the marriage can be saved.

Your husband may have stopped asking for sex because he believes your sex life cannot be saved.

I know differently. God can redeem your marital intimacy. I know it from the Word of God. I know it from personal experience. I know it from the testimonies of others. It is the result of the gospel saturating our lives.

If your husband has stopped asking, and you are relieved because you don't really want to have sex anyway, reconsider that approach. Your husband likely still desires you. His sex drive is still hungry and needs to be fed.

It's not about physical release. *You*'re what he wants, not just sex.

It may be a struggle to figure out why you are not interested, to deal with the physical or emotional issues preventing you from enjoying that kind of intimacy. It may be uncomfortable and make you feel vulnerable. It may take time.

But don't let your husband give up … on you, your sex life, your marriage. See his desire for you as a good thing, a God-given thing.

Maybe it's your turn to ask him, "Can we work on our sex life?"

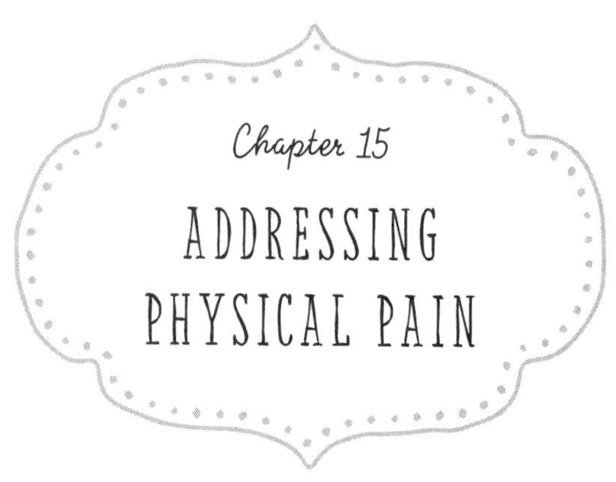

Chapter 15
ADDRESSING PHYSICAL PAIN

I wish I could say that God is completely opposed to any and all pain. But when you read the story of God's people, you find He's not against letting us suffer through pain for His higher purposes. This life is going to have some pain, but God will help us bear it.

However, sexual pain is not in that category. When it comes to sexual intimacy, God is definitely in favor of health and pleasure. There isn't some higher purpose in physically hurting when you don't need to. Let life hand you lemons when it must, but sex with your husband should be more like chocolate. Right?

> [Jesus] had compassion on them and healed their sick.
>
> Matthew 14:14

What to Do When Sex Is Painful

Here I am, encouraging wives to have great intimate encounters with their husbands. But for some women, intercourse is like inserting a serrated knife into your ear—or worse. Sex flat-out hurts.

This is absolutely not an area in which "No Pain, No Gain"

applies. Sex is not supposed to be physically painful. If it is, do not grit your teeth and bear it. Treat it like any other instance of pain in your body. If you had ongoing migraines, you'd try to find out why and treat them. If you had excruciating back pain, you'd see your doctor, a chiropractor, or a massage therapist. If you had sharp pangs every time you walked, you wouldn't stop walking altogether or decide that painful walking was your personal normal. You'd say to yourself, "Hey, what's up? Walking isn't supposed to hurt!"

God designed sex in marriage to provide intimacy and pleasure. That is what He desires for you. So what can you do to address pain during intercourse?

Examination. Visit your doctor and see if there's a physical reason for your pain. Cervical structure, low estrogen, and other factors can negatively impact your comfort during intercourse. Physical causes of sexual pain can be addressed.

After childbirth, intercourse with my husband felt like having a scythe inserted vaginally. At my third visit to the gynecologist, the physician's assistant realized that my estrogen was especially low. She prescribed a cream, and *voila!* Pain alleviated. It was a relief to me and my husband that I could engage in intimate encounters without wincing, crying buckets, and begging (internally) for him to finish. Thank goodness we discovered the physical cause and treated it.

Preparation. If physical factors are not to blame, it could be your husband is entering your body too soon. A woman needs adequate lubrication and swelling to receive a penis without discomfort. The inner vaginal lips (or labia minora) swell to perhaps three times their regular size as arousal causes blood flow to this area. If the woman is not moist enough or swollen enough, her body requires more preparation. Preparation = foreplay.

Allow yourself time to become sufficiently aroused. If necessary, designate a specified amount of time for foreplay. Tell hubby you need fifteen minutes of love play before entry. Or a certain number of romantic songs playing in the background can be your timer. Make sure you are ready for your husband's penis. If you are, it will likely feel quite good when he enters.

Lubrication. It can be difficult, at times, to produce enough lubrication on your own. Perhaps it's a time of the month when hormones are less cooperative, or you don't have sufficient time in the schedule for long foreplay, or aging is playing its part in slowing down the juices. Whatever the reason, purchase a lubricant and keep it near your bed. Try different brands to find the one you like best. You can apply the lubricant yourself or ask your hubby to do so (a request he'd likely oblige).

Moisture in the vaginal area assists with stimulation and pleasure. Your husband's fondling may not feel good without that wetness. If you aren't producing it on your own, don't worry about it. Just apply lubrication.

Experimentation. Find out what feels good to you. A lot of women who claim they don't like sex have merely accepted the method used by their husbands. If what he does doesn't feel good, try different ways of touching each other, different positions, or different times for entry or ways of thrusting. This isn't a perfect-on-the-first-try activity. Explore each other's bodies and learn what's enjoyable.

Prior to childbirth, I had a tilted uterus, and sex often felt more comfortable when my husband entered my vagina from behind. A little experimentation led us to discover a position that kept me from experiencing pain and intensified my pleasure. Of course, my enjoyment made the encounter more enjoyable for my husband as well. Free yourself to find out what brings you pleasure and what brings pain so you can pursue the former and avoid the latter.

Communication. Talk to your husband about what feels good and what doesn't. If you begin to feel discomfort or pain, let him know. He isn't a mind reader. Most men are not so absorbed by their own desire for climax that they don't care about injuring their wives. Loving husbands want their wives to gain pleasure from having sex with them. So communicate.

This may mean piping up verbally during the event to say, "Ooh, that doesn't feel good. How about this?" Or it may mean guiding his hand or his penis where you want it. It can also entail sitting down outside the bedroom and having a heart-to-heart conversation about the pain you experience and your desire to experience pleasure instead. Your husband will probably be happy to discuss options for accomplishing that goal.

Habituation. Sex needs to happen with some regularity for pain or soreness to be avoided. If I try to run five miles, my legs are going to scream bloody murder at me, and I will awaken the next morning barely able to move. If I don't run again until three months later, it will still hurt like the dickens. But if I run today, tomorrow, the next day, and so on, before I know it I will be able to run five miles with a runner's high instead of a weakling's cramping.

Some women experience pain because they do not engage in sex often enough for their muscles to adapt. Vaginas stretch a little with use. The vagina will still be tight enough to cause pleasure for the man, but it needs to remain elastic enough to respond. If sex hurts and you don't have sex again for three months, it will likely hurt just as much the next time. Making sex a habit gets your body used to the physical activity, increasing the likelihood that you will enjoy the experience.

Sex isn't supposed to hurt. If one of these reasons is causing the problem, address it immediately. Bring your husband in on the deal and enlist his help.

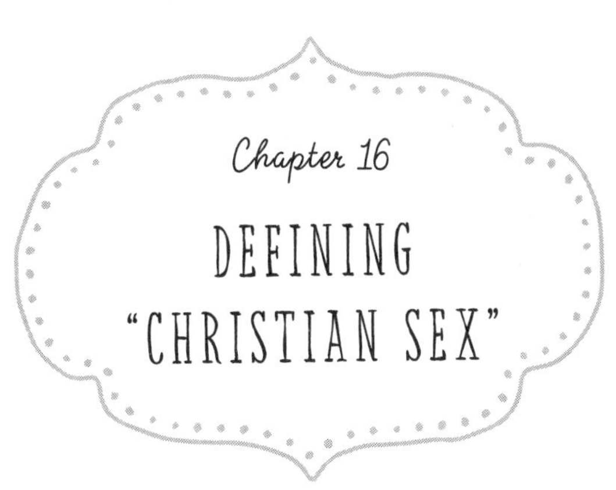

Chapter 16
DEFINING "CHRISTIAN SEX"

The clearest way of expressing my mission in writing a Christian sex book (and blog) is: "Christians need to reclaim sexuality."

Satan and the world have tried to make it theirs—a twisted version of what God created. It's not theirs. It belongs to God and to His people. To married Christians. At least the best sex does … the sex in which a couple pleases each other, expresses covenant love, and grows intimacy.

But what is "Christian sex"? What does our spiritual faith have to do with physical pleasure?

Quite a lot, actually.

> As a bridegroom rejoices over his bride,
> so will your God rejoice over you.
>
> Isaiah 62:5

Godly Sex Is Complex

In one sense, sex is simple. Intercourse requires the couple to insert Tab A into Slot B, remove, and repeat. A healthy sexual relationship requires much more.

Godly sex is complex because there are so many ways in which Satan attacks us in our sexual lives—with poor attitudes, annoying and serious problems, and complacency. Barriers to a healthy relationship primarily exist in one of these three areas.

Unhealthy attitude. This is where healthy sex *must* begin. You can hear oodles and oodles of fabulous fixes and techniques, but if one spouse approaches the other and marital intimacy with an unhealthy attitude, such ideas won't bring about a fulfilling relationship.

The biggest barrier to a good attitude is self. It can be the self-pleasuring of a mate who spends hours looking at online pornography, the self-focus of being too tired or too body conscious to make love, or the self-preservation instinct of someone who was molested in their childhood years. A healthy sexual relationship must begin with prioritizing relational intimacy above one's self.

Let me be clear here: These reasons for lack of sexual intimacy are not all selfish, but they are about self. For some, putting the marriage first means a simple attitude adjustment; for others it requires deep self-examination or therapy to heal from a painful history.

Perhaps the toughest situations I hear about are those in which one spouse has worked hard to have a great attitude toward sexual intimacy in marriage and the other spouse is a selfish blockhead. No amount of sex education will turn a selfish person into a terrific lover, because godly sexuality isn't ultimately about arousal or orgasm; it's about expressing and fostering mutual intimacy through deep physical contact.

Specific sexual problems. Some people want a better sex life, but they have specific issues that need to be addressed. Perhaps a spouse has low desire, difficulty with arousal, a pornography addiction, physical exhaustion, interrupting kids, a lack of knowledge about the human body. There's a myriad of barriers to a fulfilling sex life that have to do with addressing something specific in the person or the relationship.

Many problems can be tackled with awareness and effort. Others require the intervention of a counselor or physician. The first step is identifying what problems you have in your relationship. Your marriage is not exactly like anyone else's. However, for nearly every problem, there is a fix. It may be a quick tweak or a long-term program to get things right, but there are couples everywhere who have overcome all kinds of difficulties to become sexually intimate and satisfied in their marriages. You can be one of them!

Don't give up on working toward something better. For instance, if your physician has dismissed your inability to become aroused, find another physician. Look for answers. Find help. Making your sex life a priority means tackling the barriers to marital intimacy.

Failure to nurture. Having planted the seed of a good attitude toward marital sexuality and then seeing sprouts come up as you deal with specific problems, married couples cannot simply relax and expect to reap a never-ending harvest of sexual satisfaction. Intimacy must be nurtured.

If couples don't make time to engage in sexuality, then work, household tasks, children, church activities, friends, recreation, and more will crowd it out. You must stay in communication with each other about what you want from your sex life. And that may change with time. What felt great five years ago may not be the same now. Moreover, physical changes in your body (pregnancy, age, etc.) may present new challenges to address.

Information and encouragement, as well as knowing and

applying the Word of God to your sex life, can help substantially. If you wistfully recall your first year of marriage being a veritable sex feast and now simply sit around and wonder what happened to the delicious goodies, you'll never achieve the long-term marital intimacy God desires for you. Nurture your relationship. And that nurturing will look different in different seasons.

I deliver information, support, a little humor, and prayers that husbands and wives will work on their intimacy and discover God's beautiful gift of sexuality in marriage. But since I cannot see directly into your sex life (nor can any author, speaker, therapist, etc.), it's up to you as a married couple to figure out where the barriers are and how you want to move past them.

If you are struggling in this area, my heart aches for you. And that makes me fall to my knees. I know that our heavenly Father wants the best for His beloved children, and that includes you. It is my sincere hope that this book and my blog will help to shine light on the blessings our Lord has for you.

The Gospel in the Bedroom

We don't usually see the words *gospel* and *bedroom* in the same sentence. Yet the gospel is the central point of Christianity. Jesus Christ, God's only Son, entered the world in human form, lived and preached among us, sacrificed Himself as the ultimate blood offering for our sins, and conquered death through His resurrection so that we can live with our Lord eternally. That is definitely good news, or "gospel," for the whole world.

The gospel calls us to higher principles, purposeful lives, and servant hearts. Often, we don't allow it to permeate every area of our lives. The gospel should impact what you choose to do with your time and money, which thoughts you dwell on and which ones you resist, how you treat your friends and the restaurant drive-through employee, and—believe it or not—how you approach the marital bedroom.

The gospel matters a great deal in every aspect of life, including the intimacy you experience with your husband. Here are a few aspects of the gospel that affect your married sex life.

Because of Christ, you can trust that God can redeem your brokenness. "In him we have redemption through his blood, the forgiveness of sins, in accordance with the riches of God's grace that he lavished on us" (Ephesians 1:7–8).

If you have sexual baggage from your past—an addiction to pornography, promiscuity before your marriage, an affair that wrecked the trust in your bedroom, or whatever other sin you can think of—Jesus Christ died for that sin. He brings forgiveness and healing when you confess and repent.

Because of Christ, you can forgive your husband and give grace. "Bear with each other and forgive one another if any of you has a grievance against someone another. Forgive as the Lord forgave you" (Colossians 3:13).

Has your husband mistreated you sexually at some time? Sought his own pleasure and ignored yours? Belittled your sexual needs? Demanded sexual satisfaction or refrained from giving himself fully? Most of us can think of a time when our husbands were selfish regarding sexuality. But regardless of what has happened in the past, you can be generous, give grace, and start over.

Give your hubby the benefit of the doubt. For instance, maybe he awakened you to have sex at 3:00 a.m. last night not because he doesn't care how exhausted you were after taking care of a sick child yesterday or working on a job project with a looming deadline; maybe he was restless and started thinking about how beautiful you are to him. We can't know our husbands' exact motives, so lean toward the most positive possibility. And forgive past sins, as you have been forgiven.

Because of Christ, you can have hope for your future. "I pray that the eyes of your heart may be enlightened in order that you may know the hope to which he has called you, the riches of his glorious inheritance in his holy people, and his incomparably great power for us who believe. That power is the same as the mighty strength he exerted when he raised Christ from the dead and seated him at his right hand in the heavenly realms" (Ephesians 1:18–20).

Think about that. The same power God used to resurrect His Son is working in your life. You have hope for better things—in the life after this one and in this life as well. We know Jesus wants our lives and marriages to be full (John 10:10), loving (Ephesians 5:2), and fulfilling (1 Corinthians 7:3). When we know that God desires for us to have intimacy in our marriage and then shares His power with us, we have hope! Maybe your sex life isn't everything it should be. Continue in prayer. Continue in faith. Continue in hope.

Because of Christ, your body has intrinsic value. "Do you not know that your bodies are temples of the Holy Spirit, who is in you, whom you have received from God? You are not your own; you were bought at a price. Therefore honor God with your body" (1 Corinthians 6:19–20).

Your body is valuable and has the capacity to honor God. The verse prior to this passage says to "flee from sexual immorality" and then gives the above reason. But if you are fleeing from sexual immorality, what should you run to? Well, to sexual morality, of course! Welcome to God's plan. You honor God with your body when you follow His plan for it in marriage, when you delight in the mate your Father has given you, when you seal your commitment and intimacy with physical bonding.

Because of Christ, you know what true love is. "A new command I give you: Love one another. As I have loved you, so you must love one another" (John 13:34).

I teared up while looking at passages for this one. There are *so many* to choose from. We know what true love looks like because Jesus modeled it for us. He was patient with disciples, gentle with sinners, humble before God, and serving and sacrificial above all. Imagine taking the perfect love of Jesus into the bedroom and being patient, gentle, serving, and sacrificial. Imagine *both* of you approaching physical intimacy that way. Now tell me how fabulous that would be for your sex life.

Because of Christ, your intimacy mirrors and symbolizes what the church has with Jesus, her Bridegroom. "'For this reason a man will leave his father and mother and be united to his wife, and the two will become one flesh.' This is a profound mystery—but I am talking about Christ and the church" (Ephesians 5:31–32).

Isn't it amazing that the Old Testament verse used to reflect Christ and the church ends with "the two will become one flesh"? The unity of a husband and wife is like Christ's unity with His people. I desire to one day have with my Lord the intimacy that mirrors the intense closeness I experience with my husband in the midst of sex. How I long for it! When I experience such pleasure and bonding with my husband, I know it is a mere foretaste of what God has waiting for us in heaven.

The gospel has implications for every aspect of our lives. Our marriages are affected by God's steadfast, redeeming love. Our physical intimacy with our mates is affected by His example and sacrifice.

We Christians need not approach the bedroom as the world does. Sex isn't merely physical or all about oneself. The apex of intimacy is not multiple orgasms or more kinky sexual acts. The goal isn't to have sex *when* we want, *with whom* we want, *however* we want, *wherever* we want without regard to others. Instead we have the ultimate: a gospel-driven life that shows a better way in every area—including the marital bedroom. And guess what? With God's perfect design, we can end up having the most amazing sex!

I pray for each married couple to experience the gospel in their bedroom—to know the overwhelming love of Christ and to share it with each other.

> "I pray that you, being rooted and established in love, may have power, together with all the Lord's holy people, to grasp how wide and long and high and deep is the love of Christ, and to know this love that surpasses knowledge—that you may be filled to the measure of all the fullness of God" (Ephesians 3:17–19).

Chapter 17
CALLING US TO MINISTRY

There is a growing awareness that individual Christians and church communities need to speak up, not merely against ungodly sexuality but also in favor of godly sexuality.

Speaking up isn't always easy. Some believe we shouldn't talk about sex because the act itself is to be between two exclusive, committed persons. But God doesn't shy away from the subject of sex. It's all through Scripture. We can have a public conversation about sex without compromising our ultimate privacy.

So let's join Peter and John in their prayer:

> Enable your servants to speak your word with great boldness.
>
> Acts 4:29

Step Up, Church, and Talk about Sex

How should Christians and the church in general address the subject of sexuality?

Take a look at the letters of Paul in the New Testament. He boldly addressed whatever issue plagued the church and refocused people on God's desire for their lives.

Wrongful thinking and behaviors regarding sex permeate our culture. From the sexually abused child to the promiscuous teen to the porn-addicted husband to the withholding wife to the married couple who struggles to connect physically, we are off target a lot. Jesus never turned a blind eye to sin and pain in His midst. It is our God-given duty to speak into others' pain and confusion, to speak for God where He has spoken, and to pass on God's desire for their lives, even in the area of sexuality.

What should this boldness look like? Ideally, churches should have a cradle-to-grave approach. Here are my suggestions for how churches can minister to people in various stages:

Children/Teens

Provide parenting classes to help families address the subject. Plenty of parents want to equip their children with a godly view of sexuality, but they simply don't know how to talk to their kids about it.

Empower youth ministry to address biblical sexuality with tweens and teens. All too often, parents resist having the subject brought up in church. Guess what? It's being brought up everywhere else your kid is. Isn't it better for our children to get information from a biblically driven youth pastor than to rely on his/her school friend or a TV show?

Host fun, well-supervised teen events. Churches can help teens by hosting events that provide opportunities to mingle and have fun without the sexual temptation that often exists in secular venues. It needs to be something that will attract teens but also keep them out of pressurized situations. For instance, when I was a teen, a couple of churches hosted dances. The likelihood of anything inappropriate happening with my date at his Mormon church's family dance was practically nil. Here's another out-of-the-box idea: What if a church rented a bunch of luxury cars and had volunteer members drive teenagers and their dates to and from local proms?

Singles

Provide pre-engagement and premarital classes and counseling. There are some excellent studies out there for dating couples. Ask most married couples if they wish they had prepared more, and they'll say yes—including in the area of sexual intimacy.

Help singles find mates. I don't believe everyone must get married or that being single is a lesser status. However, 1 Corinthians 7:9 says, "It is better to marry than to burn with passion." And, although marriage rates in the United States are declining,[22] most people still want to be married at some point. Hey, the best thing the church ever did for my sex life was to introduce me to my husband. But many single Christians today have few options.

What can churches do? They can offer area-wide singles events. I'm not suggesting some Christian version of *The Bachelor* or *The Dating Game*. Such events shouldn't be meat markets, but rather worship, fellowship, or Bible studies that allow singles to gather and get to know one another. Love can take it from there.

Marrieds

Make marriage classes, retreats, and seminars routine. In addition to in-depth scriptural and theological studies, churches should teach on the practical application of God's Word. Look for biblically based marriage studies or find couples with knowledge to share.

Don't skip the sex part! This is part B of the above suggestion. I was once told by another marriage blogger that churches often skip the sex lesson in a marriage series—perhaps because the topic is considered too sensitive. That tidbit of information had me V8-headsmacking the rest of the day. God wants married couples to have growing marriages and great sex! Let's support healthy marriages by helping couples do exactly that.

Financially support marriage ministries. Many quality marriage resources can only continue through outside financial support, and churches can make that a goal of their budget.

Provide babysitting services to married couples with children. One of the hardest periods for marital intimacy is when the kids are young. A group of church members (e.g., youth, "Golden Agers," singles) could provide babysitting as a ministry. Or a church could establish a babysitting co-op in which couples keep one another's kids at times and then get their own date nights.

Miscellaneous

Take a sex survey of your church and present your findings. Oftentimes, we don't know that church members are struggling with sexuality. Who's going to stand up on Sunday morning and say, "Could you address biblical sexuality? Because I ain't gettin' any at home!" We can awaken the attention of church leaders and members by asking for anonymous input about where they are thriving and where they need help.

Be specific. Churches often address sexuality at too high a level. For singles, we hear, "God wants you to stay pure." Yes, He does. But be specific about how a sexually ramped-up seventeen-year-old boy can stay cool when a hot girl throws herself at him. Or how a twenty-three-year-old single woman can wait another seven years before her libido sees daylight. For the marrieds, it isn't enough to say, "God wants you to have a good sex life." How does a husband figure out how to pleasure his wife to climax? How can a woman deal with her lagging interest in sex? How can a couple move beyond negative sexual histories? Be specific.

Bring in special speakers. Christian colleges and universities often have marriage and family therapy or Christian ministry departments with qualified experts. There are also writers, bloggers, counselors, and speakers who address this subject.

Offer couples counseling. Couples counseling should be available to dating teens, couples in serious relationships, engaged couples, and married couples. The singles may need a session or two to learn strategies for stopping sexual activity before it starts, while a married couple may need to address a lack of intimacy or physical barriers to satisfying sex. If the church does not have the wherewithal to offer such counseling, it can subsidize another church's counseling center or a Christian-based counseling practice.

Plug into ministries that help those who need special care. Has a child been sexually abused? Is a husband dealing with a porn addiction? Is a couple dealing with adultery? Such issues go beyond typical couples counseling. Find ministries that address specific issues.

Look for experts in your midst. That physician who attends your church? The labor and delivery nurse? The psychologist or counselor? The recovering sex addict? The woman who was sexually abused as a child and found healing? The couple who lived through an affair and now have a thriving marriage? They all have something to offer. Ask how they are willing to help support healthy and godly sex lives for church members.

Maintain a quality library with helpful resources on biblical sexuality. There are many Christian-based books and video and audio series available, but cost can be prohibitive for families. Churches could purchase resources, then let families know what's available.

No one church can offer all of this, so we must rely on one another in the larger church body. But each church can address godly sexuality throughout the seasons of life by offering biblical knowledge, specific information, relationship support, and prayer for the purity and intimacy of their members.

What does your church do to boldly address biblical sexuality? What can you do?

ACKNOWLEDGMENTS

When I answered the Holy Spirit's nudging and started a blog about marriage and sexuality, I had no idea God would use my little voice to speak into the lives of so many and to help them experience the blessings from pursuing sex in marriage by God's design.

This mission and journey are not mine alone. My heartfelt thanks go out to:

My Lord and Savior. "To whom shall I go? You have the words of eternal life" (John 6:68). Thank you for using my story, my marriage, and my life for your higher purposes.

My partners in ministry. I could name many other like-minded voices, but thanks in particular to Sheila Wray Gregoire and Julie Sibert for your early and ongoing help and to Debi Walter for inspiring the chapter on The Gospel in the Bedroom.

My illustrator. Matt, I thank God for giving you such talent, and I thank you for using your talent to render such simple, beautiful drawings.

My agent. Thanks for hunting me down, Greg, and believing in me. I'll be forever grateful.

My publisher. Thanks to BroadStreet for championing this project, being such a joy to work with, and fixing all my oopses to make this book flow smoothly.

My readers and followers. Thanks for keeping me on my toes with great questions, powerful testimonies, and encouragement.

My family. Thanks for not freaking out when I said I'd been called a "sexpert" and for your loving support.

My husband (whom my readers know as "Spock"). You've lived with me through the good, the bad, and the "you rock my world!" years. I love you more now than ever. (Psst, race you to the bedroom!)

NOTES

1 Elizabeth Barrett Browning, "Sonnet 43," in *Sonnets from the Portuguese* (New York: Harper, 1932).
2 Letter from Abigail Adams to John Adams, December 23, 1782, in *Adams Family Papers: An Electronic Archive* (Massachusetts Historical Society). http://www.masshist.org/digitaladams/.
3 Emily Temple, "The Torrid Love Letters of Famous Authors," *The Atlantic* (February 14, 2012), http://www.theatlantic.com/entertainment/archive /2012/02/the-torrid-love-letters-of-famous-authors/253089/.
4 SLC to Olivia L. Langdon, January 7, 1869, Rockford, IL (UCCL 00220). In *Mark Twain's Letters, 1869*, ed. by Victor Fischer, Michael B. Frank, and Dahlia Armon, Mark Twain Project Online (Berkeley, Los Angeles, CA: University of California Press, 1992, 2007), accessed January 26, 2016, http://www.marktwainproject.org/xtf/vi ew?docId=letters/UCCL00220. xml;style=let ter;brand=mtp,.
5 Robert Browning to Elizabeth Barrett Browning, The Browning Letters, accessed January 26, 2016, http://digitalcollections.baylor.edu/cdm /compoundobject/collection/ab-letters/id/1966/show/1960/rec/1.
6 William J. Bennett, *The Book of Man: Readings on the Path to Manhood* (Nashville, TN: Thomas Nelson, 2011).
7 Gerard W. Gawalt, My *Dear President: Letters between Presidents and Their Wives*, (New York: Black Dog & Leventhal, 2005).
8 Letter: Winston Churchill to Clementine Churchill, September 15, 1909, Churchill and the Great Republic (A Library of Congress Interactive Exhibition, Text Version), accessed January 27, 2016, http://www.loc.gov /exhibits/churchill/interactive/_html/wc0046.html.
9 Robert Browning to Elizabeth Barrett Browning, The Browning Letters.
10 *When Harry Met Sally*, directed by Rob Reiner (1989), film.
11 *Theatre Arts* 39:12 (1955): 8.

12 "Sexual Positions in Your Marriage: Hey, I'm a Housewife, Not a Gymnast." Intimacy in Marriage. May 18, 2011; http://intimacyinmarriage.com/2011/05/18/sexual-positions-in-your-marriage-hey-im-a-housewife-not-a-gymnast/.

13 Gallup, GG, Jr., RL Burch, and SM Platek. "Does Semen Have Antidepressant Properties?" National Center for Biotechnology Information. Accessed January 29, 2016. http://www.ncbi.nlm.nih.gov/pubmed/12049024.

14 Sophia Breene, "Superfood or Supergross? The Truth About Semen," Greatist (February 19, 2013), http://greatist.com/health/nutrition-of-semen.

15 Sheila Wray Gregoire, *31 Days to Great Sex* (Winnipeg: Word Alive Press. 2013).

16 Ed Wheat and Gaye Wheat, *Intended for Pleasure* (Old Tappan, NJ: Fleming H. Revell, 1981), 55.

17 "Larry-Boy and the Rumour Weed," *VeggieTales*, DVD, directed by Phil Vischer (Chicago, IL: Big Idea Entertainment, 1999).

18 "Seal," in *Baker's Evangelical Dictionary of Biblical Theology*. Bible Study Tools, accessed February 1, 2016, http://www.biblestudytools.com/dictionaries/bakers-evangelical-dictionary/seal.html.

19 Mohammed Mirza, "Porn-induced Erectile Dysfunction (PIED)," SexualHealthMen.com (April 15, 2014), http://sexualhealthmen.com/blog/porn-induced-erectile-dysfunction-pied/; see also Matt Fradd, "Does Porn Cause Erectile Dysfunction? Yes. Here's Why," Covenant Eyes (February 27, 2015), http://www.covenanteyes.com/2015/02/27/porn-cause-erectile-dysfunction/.

20 Sheila Wray Gregoire, *The Good Girl's Guide to Great Sex: (and You Thought Bad Girls Have All the Fun)* (Grand Rapids, MI: Zondervan, 2012).

21 http://www.medicalnewstoday.com/releases/35663.php.

22 Susan Braudy, "He's Woody Allen's Not-So-Silent Partner," *New York Times* (August 21, 1977).

23 Wendy Wang and Kim Parker, "Record Share of Americans Have Never Married," Pew Research Centers Social Demographic Trends Project RSS (September 14, 2014), http://www.pewsocialtrends.org/2014/09/24/record-share-of-americans-have-never-married/.

ABOUT THE AUTHOR

J. Parker has been writing at the *Hot, Holy & Humorous* blog since 2010, using a biblical perspective and a blunt sense of humor to foster godly sexuality. Her mission to encourage sex in marriage by God's design was inspired by her personal story and God's beautiful nudging.

She's been married for twenty-three years to a faithful and far less talkative husband, has two teenage sons who are proud of what Mom does and never want to read a word of it, and lives in Friendswood, Texas, a bedroom community between Houston and Galveston. She holds a bachelor's degree in history and a master's degree in counseling.

When she isn't writing or speaking about godly sex or conducting "research" with her husband, J writes teen fiction; hugs, disciplines, or cracks jokes with her kids (whichever is needed in the moment); and daydreams about having a personal chef and an on-call massage therapist.

You can find out more about J's ministry and follow her blog at www.hotholyhumorous.com.